The Official
HEAVY METAL
BOOK OF LISTS

The Official
HEAVY METAL
BOOK OF LISTS

Eric Danville

Backbeat
Books

An Imprint of Hal Leonard Corporation
New York

Published in 2009 by Backbeat Books
An Imprint of Hal Leonard Corporation
7777 West Bluemound Road
Milwaukee, WI 53213

Trade Book Division Editorial Offices
19 West 21st Street, New York, NY 10010

Printed in the United States of America

Book design by Snow Creative Services

Illustrations by Cliff Mott

Library of Congress Cataloging-in-Publication Data

Danville, Eric.
  The official heavy metal book of lists / Eric Danville.
      p. cm.
  ISBN 978-0-87930-983-1 (alk. paper)
  1. Heavy metal (Music)--Miscellanea. I. Title.
  ML3534.D36 2009
  781.66--dc22
                              2009031940

www.backbeatbooks.com

This book is dedicated to Nüdl, the coolest poodle on the planet.

CONTENTS

Foreword by Lemmy   xiii
Preface   xv

1. D/A (Drugs and Alcohol)   1
Rock Bottom: 10 Metalheads Arrested for Being Drunk in Public   1
50 Heavy Metal Drinking Songs   3
73 Metal Bands with Druggy or Boozy Names   4
41 Smack-Shootin', Coke-Snortin', Hopped-Up, Tweaked-Out Metal Tunes   6
Born to Be Wired: 10 Heavy Metal Drug Busts   8
Richard Christy of Iced Earth and *The Howard Stern Show*'s Top 5 Heavy
    Metal Lyrics You'd Most Likely Hear Referred To at a Keg Party in
    Uniontown, Kansas, in 1989   11
12 Fatal Drug Overdoses and One Drug OD Who Came Back from
    the Dead   12
We Have a Drink or Two...Well, Maybe Three: How 11 Metalheads
    Knock 'Em Back   13
Honey 1%'er of the Cycle Sluts from Hell's 5 Best Places to Drink and
    Listen to Metal in New York City in the '80s   16
Kittie's Top 6 "Get Drunk for Under $30" Wines   19
"Saucy" Jack Bastard's 12 Drinks That'll Bang Your Head   20

2. O (Occult)   25
Finally! Proof Positive That (at Least) 8 Heavy Metal Acts Indulge in
    Devil Worship, Drug Use, and Sexual Perversity   25
Dr. Phibes of Blood Farmers' Evolution of Occult Metal in 13 Songs   27
7 Links Between Led Zeppelin and the Occult   31
8 Metal Bands Who Got Their Names from Horror Movies   33
A Nasty Hobbit: 15 Metal Bands Who Got Their Names from
    J.R.R. Tolkien   34
Body Piercing Saved My Life Author Andrew Beaujon's List of
    9 Christian Metal Band Names, Translated   37

Contents

A Kiss Is Just a Kiss: The Supposedly Evil Meanings of 3 Metal
Bands' Names   38

The Names of 10 of Alice Cooper's Snakes   39

Shabbos Bloody Shabbos: 37 Headbangin' Jews   41

Back in Unblack: 33 Christian Rock Bands Who Shout at the Devil   42

Spinal Tap Meets *The Mummy*: Mike McPadden's 13 Favorite, Absolutely
Killer Heavy Metal Horror Movies . . .   42

. . . and 12 Headbanging Cameos in Non-Horror Movies   46

Pure Fucking Armageddon: The Norwegian Black Metal Body Count   48

3. V (Violence)   53

Peter Grant's Greatest Hits: 7 People Assaulted by the Manager of Led
Zeppelin (and One Very Honorable Mention)   53

11 Heavy Metal Gigs That Ended in Riots (and Only 4 Were
Guns N' Roses!)   55

51 Awesomely Violent Band Names   58

28 Bands with Bloody Names   59

12 People Who Found Themselves on the Business End of Sharon Osbourne   59

Metal Poet Yoko Kinzoku's History of Van Halen Feuds in Haiku   63

7 Metalheads Who Were Injured Onstage   65

126 Metal Band Names That Have to Do with . . . Death or Dying!   68

9 Metal Suicides   69

3 Metal Bands Cleared of Causing Someone's Suicide or Murder   70

25 Bands Named After . . . Mental Defect or Disease!   71

6 Metalheads Who Have Worn Straitjackets   72

12 Metal Songs About Serial Killers   72

8 Metalheads Who Were Murdered   73

Under My Wheels: 13 Metalheads Who Died in Vehicle Accidents   74

Metal's 5 Gnarliest Deaths   75

The 5 Dead Spinal Tap Drummers   75

Dave Brockie (a.k.a. Oderus Urungus of Gwar)'s 10 Sickest Things
to Ever Happen at a Gwar Show   76

Pirate Radio Pioneer Dave Rabbit's *Radio First Termer* Playlist   79

4 Metal Bands with an Unusual, Coincidental Connection to 9/11
(and One Honorable Mention)   83

48 Metal Songs That Clear Channel Communications "Suggested"
Their Radio Stations Avoid Playing After the September 11, 2001,
Terror Attacks (And One Honorable Mention)   84
8 Heavy Metal Songs the Government Has Used to Torture Prisoners
at Abu Ghraib and Guantánamo Bay   86
William Murderface of Dethklok's Top 5 Most Metal Civil War Generals   88

4. X (Sex/Obscenity)   91

10 Heavy Metal Celebrity Sex Tapes   91
52 Band Names About . . . Pussy!   94
Love at First Sting: 9 Heavy Metal Bitch Magnets . . .   95
. . . and 3 Bitchin' Heavy Metal Heartbreakers   96
10 Smoking Hot Heavy Metal Video Vixens   96
A Fine Line Between Stupid and Clever: 11 Bands Whose "Controversial"
Album Covers Were Banned, Censored, or Changed   98
25 Band Names About . . . Well . . . You Figure It Out   100
Hammers of the Gods: 28 Well-Hung Metalheads   101
Ken Susi of Unearth's Top 10 Spots to Fuck Groupies   102
Comedian and That Metal Show Co-Host Jim Florentine's
5 Motörhead Songs to Fuck Your Chick To   102
You've Got Another Thing Coming: 6 Openly Gay Metalheads   103
70 X-Rated Band Names   104
3 Heavy Metal Performers Arrested for Sex Crimes   105
Dr. Dot's 8 Heavy Metal Hardbodies   106
Your Time Is Gonna Come: 20 Bands Singing the Praises of Necrophilia   109
21 Band Names About . . . Ass!   110
5 Porn Stars with Metal-Inspired Stage Names . . .   111
. . . and One Metal Band That Returned the Favor   111
Director Matt Zane of Society 1 Remembers 25 Metalheads Who
Appeared in His Porn Movies   111
4 Heavy Metal Non-Sex Porn Film Cameos   115
Jasmin St. Claire's 10 Reasons Metal Dudes Are So Hot . . .   115
. . . and 10 Reasons Why Metal Chicks Are So Hot   116
Whole Lotta Continua: Sasha Grey's 16 Favorite Metal Albums 'n' Shit   118

5. Noise

5. Noise	**123**
19 Unlikely Heavy Metal Pairings (and One Honorable Mention)	123
Gonna Make Your Ears Bleed: The World's 3 Loudest Heavy Metal Bands	125
John 5 of Marilyn Manson's Top 10 Favorite Concerts and Tours of All Time	126
Unusual Versions of Led Zeppelin Songs Performed Live by Ex-Members	127
Welcome to My Nightmare: Eric Danville's 5 Most Wanted Metal Bootlegs	127
11 "Real" Musicians Who Have Played with Spinal Tap	129
Give the Drummer Some: 6 Outrageous Drum Solo Stunts	129
Metal Up Your Glasnost: The First 6 Western Heavy Metal Bands to Play Rock Festivals in Russia	132
12 Heavy Metal Concept Albums, and Their Concepts	132
Dave Thompson's 9 Subversive Metal Influences	133
Dave Depraved of Blood Farmers' 6 Songs That Were Metal Before You Were Metal	136
15 Metal Bands Who Used to Play It Punk	138
It's Fuckin' Metal, Dude!: 108 Genres and Subgenres, A to Z	138
My Suite Satan: 5 Heavy Metal Bands Who Have Performed Live with a Symphony Orchestra	140
21 All-Chick Metal Cover Bands	140
Steph Paynes of Lez Zeppelin's 12 Things You Should Know if You Want to Play Guitar Like Jimmy Page	142
The Song Retains the Name: 15 Unusual Metal Cover Bands	143
Ice-T of Body Count's 11 Favorite Heavy Metal Bands	146
Joel McIver of *Record Collector* Magazine's List of 10 Most Valuable Heavy Metal Vinyls	146
9 Non-Metal Bands That Do a Song Called "Heavy Metal"	147
False Metal: 6 Mainstream Artists Who Have Covered Metal Songs	148
Thick as a Brick: 21 Years of Metal Grammy Winners	150
100 (Mainly) Instrumental Heavy Metal Acts	151
Listen to the Flower People: 13 Weird-Ass Heavy Metal Instruments	153
Crazy Train: 10 Unusual Metal Bands	154
Pete Fry of Rockarma and FarCry's 6 Songs That Almost Made Me Quit Playing Guitar	157
12 Gibson Flying V Guitarists	158
10 Fun Facts About the Gibson EDS 1275 Double Neck Guitar	159
29 Metalheads with Signature Model Guitars	160

Mike Edison's 5 Greatest Heavy Metal Gimmicks (and One Truly
    Pathetic Attempt)   162
2008 World Air Guitar Champion Hot Lixx Hulahan's 8 Tips
    for Successful Air Guitar   164
11 Things That Have Happened Between the Release of Guns N' Roses'
    The Spaghetti Incident? and *Chinese Democracy*   166

6. On the Road   169

The 7 Wonders of the Metal World   169
Ron "Bumblefoot" Thal's 10 Lamest Things Anyone Said to Me
    Right Before Playing a Show   171
6 Songs About Roadies   173
Alex Wade of Whitechapel's 10 Things I've Learned While Being
    a Touring Musician   174
Deal with the Devil: 12 Weird Requests Made in Heavy Metal
    Contract Riders   175
Phil Campbell of Motörhead's List of 6 Things You'll Never See in a
    Motörhead Dressing Room . . .   177
. . . and 11 Things That Annoy Me About Hotels   178
Eat 'Em and Smile: Food Demands from 9 Heavy Metal Contract Riders   178
Jan Kuehnemund of Vixen's List of 10 Reasons Why I Need My Own
    Hotel Room on the Road . . .   181
. . . and the First 12 Things I Do as Soon as I Get In It   182
Eric Adams of Manowar's 10 Favorite Metal Cities   183
Bob Gorman (a.k.a. Muzzle Slave) of Gwar's 10 Weirdest Places
    Gwar Have Performed   184
17 Metalheads' Stage Names and How They Got Them   186
Evan Seinfeld of Biohazard's Top 5 Famous Heavy Metal Cars,
    Top 5 Factory Muscle Cars, and One Honorable Mention   190

7. Whole Lotta Lists   193

Special When Lit: Aaron Lefkove's 7 Wonders of Heavy Metal Pinball   193
20 Heavy Metal Party Bands with Fucking Awesome Names   194
Brandon Patton of Echoes of Eternity's 3 Reasons Why Being
    a Professional Musician Sucks   195
Gimme Some Money: 12 Heavy Metal Pitchmen and What They Shill   196
But Wait! There's More! 32 Great Moments in Kiss Merchandising   198

Contents

Stay with Me, Baby: Lita Ford and Jim Gillette's 12 Ways to Make
    a Metal Marriage Last   199
Hail, Seitan! 30 Heavy Metal Vegans and Vegetarians   200
Six Feet Over: 34 Towering Metalheads   201
Little Big Men: 9 Metalheads Who Are 5´6˝ or Under   202
20 Metalheads Who Should *Never* Wear Spandex, Corsets, or Fishnet . . .   204
. . . and 20 Who Should Never Leave Home Without Them   204
Otep Shamaya's 10 Most Recently Read Books   206
4 Metalheads Who Have Done Musical Theater   206
The Good, the Bad, and the Ugly: Alex Mitchell of Circus of Power's
    Top 3 Metal Moments   208
Heavy Metal Parking Lot Director Jeff Krulik's 12 Movies with
    a Metal Attitude   209
21 Hair Metal Video Fashion Tips   212
36 Hair Metal Video Clichés   213
The *Colbert Report*'s Resident Rocker Jason Baker's 6 Incidences
    of Heavy Metal Hair Loss   215
Masters of Reality: 12 Heavy Metal Reality Shows   216
11 Notable Cameos in Heavy Metal Videos   217
Heavy Mental: 22 Fictitious and Parody Bands   219
10 Things Ronnie James Dio Is Older Than   223
Ted Nugent by the Numbers   223

Acknowledgments   229
Bibliography   231

FOREWORD by Lemmy

motörhead

Hello everyone, hello,
Here is a book of lists,
the most impressive of which is 80% to
starboard. I hope you will be ~~very~~ duly
excited by the research which has
obviously been long and arduous, the layout
which has been meticulous, and the paper,
which is white.

My own lists are far more mundane:
Girls, guitars, things to do, things to ignore,
things to pretend you never saw etc.

As a reference this is probably a great
asset to archivists, or just plain collectors.
I myself am a great reference book collector, but
funnily enough there is no list of them!
I thoroughly recommend this small tome,
and the best of UKness to you all.

Let me leave you with a question to
ponder: what's another word for 'thesaurus'.

Ha! Ys.

Lemmy xx

PREFACE

Heavy metal's first great list was written twenty-five years ago by the Parents Music Resource Center (PMRC). The history and impact of the PMRC are well-documented, but briefly, that well-connected, politically ambitious "consumerist" group was founded after Mrs. Tipper Gore—wife of then-Senator Albert Gore of Tennessee—listened to the Prince song "Darling Nikki," which contained a reference to masturbation. (Another member, Treasury Secretary James Baker's wife Susan, was similarly shocked to hear her daughter singing the lyrics to "Like a Virgin" by Madonna.)

Along with the National Parent-Teacher Association, the PMRC called upon the Recording Industry Association of America (RIAA) to give parents a consumer-friendly means of identifying rock records unsuitable for minors—a ratings system based on lyrical content: **D/A for drug and alcohol references, O for occult, V for violence, and S for sex or obscenity**. To demonstrate the need for the ratings system, the PMRC collected some of the songs they felt should carry these ratings and created the first really official heavy metal list . . .

The PMRC's "Filthy Fifteen" (and Their Lyrics Ratings)

1. "Eat Me Alive"—Judas Priest, X
2. "Bastard"—Mötley Crüe, V
3. "Darling Nikki"—Prince, X
4. "Sugar Walls"—Sheena Easton, X
5. "(Animal) Fuck Like a Beast"—W.A.S.P., X
6. "Into the Coven"—Mercyful Fate, O
7. "Strap On Robby Baby"—Vanity, X
8. "High 'n' Dry"—Def Leppard, D/A
9. "We're Not Gonna Take It"—Twisted Sister, V
10. "Dress You Up"—Madonna, X
11. "She Bop"—Cyndi Lauper, X
12. "Let Me Put My Love Into You"—AC/DC, X

13. "Trashed"—Black Sabbath, D/A
14. "In My House"—Mary Jane Girls, X
15. "Possessed"—Venom, O

Fueled by a well-organized, media-savvy dog-and-pony show outlining death, damnation, and the downfall of the American family, the PMRC's campaign against rock and roll, like similar crusades against comic books in the '50s, snowballed and, in August 1985, resulted in what became known as the "Porn Rock" hearings. Testimony discussing the labeling system and its ramifications was given before the Senate Commerce, Science, and Transportation Committee by members of the PMRC, supporters of the labeling system, and three high-profile opponents: John Denver, Frank Zappa and Dee Snider of Twisted Sister.

Whether you support the rights of parents to monitor what their kids listen to or hate government intrusion into any aspect of individual life, it's important to remember the upshot of the 1985 Porn Rock hearings: the RIAA's compromise to "voluntarily" place stickers reading "Parental Advisory: Explicit Content" on those releases they deemed necessary. Almost as if to demonstrate how far you could go to protect America's youth, the label even appeared (sarcastically, I imagine) on the cover of Zappa's album *Jazz from Hell*—which contained no lyrics at all. The PMRC-inspired labeling initiative continues to this day and is still lauded by the RIAA on their website.

When my editor first mentioned the idea of me doing the follow up to *The Official Punk Rock Book of Lists* with a heavy metal edition, its hook seemed obvious. In honor of the PMRC—and to remind people that in these days of initiatives like the Children's Internet Protection Act, the Library Services and Technology Act, and the Patriot Act, government-sanctioned censorship still hasn't gone away—the first four chapters of *The Official Heavy Metal Book of Lists* are based on their ratings system. But to kick things off, I'd like to present a list highlighting the efforts of the man who definitely means it when he sings, "I wanna rock!"

8 Totally Fucking Awesome Dee Snider Quotes from the 1985 Porn Rock Hearings

1. "I am thirty years old, I am married, I have a three-year-old son. I was born and raised a Christian and I still adhere to those principles. Believe it or not, I do not smoke, I do not drink, and I do not do drugs. I do play in and write the songs for a rock and roll band named Twisted Sister that is classified as heavy metal, and I pride myself on writing songs that are consistent with my above-mentioned beliefs."

2. "As the creator of 'Under the Blade,' I can say categorically that the only sadomasochism, bondage, and rape in this song is in the mind of Ms. Gore."

3. "The video 'We're Not Gonna Take It' was simply meant to be a cartoon with human actors playing variations on the Roadrunner/Wile E. Coyote theme. Each stunt was selected from my extensive personal collection of cartoons."

4. "Parents can thank the PMRC for reminding them that there is no substitute for parental guidance. But that is where the PMRC's job ends."

5. "As a parent myself and as a rock fan, I know that when I see an album cover with a severed goat's head in the middle of a pentagram between a woman's legs, that is not the kind of album I want my son to be listening to."

6. "Being a parent is not a reasonable thing. It is a very hard thing. I am a parent and I know. . . . It is not just always a cute baby. There is a lot of labor, a lot of time, and a lot of effort that goes into it. It is not totally pleasurable."

7. "I do not put anything down on a record that I cannot stand behind 100 percent. I do not sing about drugs, sex, alcohol. I do not advocate sexism, the use of drugs and drinking, and so I do not write about those things. I only write about things I believe in."

8. "I am trying to get adults to see that heavy metal is not totally a bad thing."

The Official
HEAVY METAL
BOOK OF LISTS

D/A
(DRUGS AND ALCOHOL)

Rock Bottom: 10 Metalheads Arrested for Being Drunk in Public

1. Ace Frehley (Kiss)

In 1983, "Space Ace," composer of the Kiss classic "Cold Gin," led New York's Finest on a high-speed car chase the wrong way on the Bronx River Expressway before crashing his DeLorean in White Plains, New York. He then had his license suspended. The incident was the inspiration for another composition, "Rock Soldiers."

2. Ozzy Osbourne (Black Sabbath)

Back in his drinking days, the Prince of Darkness had some amazing run-ins with the law. During a photo shoot in February 1982, Ozzy was picked up by San Antonio cops after he was caught taking a piss on the Alamo—in drag, wearing one of his wife Sharon's dresses. Two years later, Memphis police hauled Ozzy in for "public intoxication" after he was spotted walking around "staggeringly drunk." Five years later a wildly fucked-up Ozzy shot and killed more than a dozen of his family's pet cats, and in a separate incident that year was arrested for domestic abuse after attempting to strangle Sharon.

3. Axl Rose (Guns N' Roses)

The baddest of rock's bad boys has been arrested almost three dozen times. One of his more interesting scuffles occurred after a 2006 gig in Stockholm, Sweden, when the band showed up at the Café Opera nightclub, ready to party. Axl spent the evening surrounded by blondes, sipping chilled Jack Daniel's until early in the morning. At some point a fight broke out, apparently between Axl and a woman in the lobby of his hotel; he was arrested at eight in the morning, violently drunk and so out of control—he punched a security guard and then bit him on the leg—that he had to be physically restrained. He paid a fine and was released the same day.

4. Richie Sambora (Bon Jovi)

Police pulled Sambora over for driving drunk in Laguna Beach, California. He accepted a plea deal of three years' probation and three months of alcohol abuse workshops and was held liable for $1,600 in court costs; as a result of the plea deal, a second drunk driving charge was dropped. Sambora had faced the possibility of additional charges of child endangerment because his ten-year-old daughter was in the car at the time, but those charges were never filed.

5. Scott Stapp (Creed)

Creed's lead singer was arrested for being drunk and disorderly at Los Angeles International Airport the day after he got married. He was released after posting $250 bail.

6. Scott Weiland (Velvet Revolver)

In 2003, Weiland was arrested in Hollywood for driving under the influence; the charges were dismissed after he successfully completed a stint in rehab. Los Angeles police arrested Weiland again in November 2007 for driving under the influence of a drug after a "non-injury" accident; Weiland took a Breathalyzer test at the scene, but refused to submit blood and urine samples after he was booked, in defiance of California state law. After entering a plea of "no contest," Weiland was sentenced to 192 hours of jail, an eighteen-month alcohol rehabilitation program, and four years' probation, and had to pay a $2,000 fine.

7. John Patrick "Midnight" McDonald Jr. (Crimson Glory)

Crimson Glory showed Midnight the door after he was arrested in Sarasota, Florida, for driving under the influence with a suspended license—and a minor in the passenger seat. His blood alcohol level was .20.

8. Clint Lowery (Korn, touring guitarist)
Following a July 2007 gig at the Hodokvas Festival in Piestany, Slovakia, Lowery was arrested on a drunk and disorderly charge after trashing his room. Lowery paid the hotel for the damage he caused, said he was sorry, and was released from custody.

9. Lori Barbero (Babes in Toyland)
The drummer drove her car through her garage and into her house.

10. Vince Neil (Mötley Crüe)
Neil served half of a thirty-day sentence and received five years' probation for vehicular manslaughter after a drunk driving accident that killed Hanoi Rocks drummer Razzle and seriously injured two other people in December 1984.

50 Heavy Metal Drinking Songs

1. "A Drinking Song"—Rivendell
2. "The Drinking Song"—Stormwitch
3. "Let's Drink"—Korpiklaani
4. "Have a Drink on Me"—AC/DC
5. "I've Been Drinking"—Ligeia
6. "Drinking Again"—Diamond Head
7. "Drinking Makes Me Smarter, I Think"—Killwhitneydead
8. "Liquor Saved Me from Sports"—Terror 2000
9. "Hell Bent for Beer"—Steelpreacher
10. "The Art of Partying"—Municipal Waste
11. "Good Times"—written by Eric Burdon, recorded by Ozzy Osbourne
12. "Beer Muscles"—Scatterbrain
13. "Whiplash Liquor"—Ugly Kid Joe
14. "Whiskey Drinkin' Woman"—Nazareth
15. "Cold Gin"—Kiss
16. "Whiskey in the Morning"—Buckcherry
17. "Lace and Whiskey"—Alice Cooper
18. "Jamaican Rum"—Philip Lynott
19. "Tequila"—Morgana Lefay
20. "I Wish You Were a Beer"—Cycle Sluts from Hell
21. "Moonshine"—Sister Whiskey
22. "Pussy Liquor"—Rob Zombie
23. "Beat, Booze, the Hookers Lose"—Dominus

24. "My Baby Ruby"—Golden Earring
25. "Forced Down Your Throat"—SS Decontrol
26. "Straight-Edge Closed Mind"—Grief
27. "Alcohaulin' Ass"—Hellyeah
28. "Armageddon Y'Know"—Cryhavoc
29. "Dick"—Realm
30. "Up An' Down"—Heavens Gate
31. "Anyone for Tinnies?"—Lawnmower Deth
32. "Dying in a Monologue"—An Early Cascade
33. "Cult of Intoxication"—Fuck Off and Die
34. "State of Control"—Barren Cross
35. "Suicide Solution"—Ozzy Osbourne
36. "Use Your Mind"—Extreme Noise Terror
37. "Dying Inside"—Saint Vitus
38. "Divine Intoxication"—Warcollapse
39. "Ocean of Tears"—Turbo
40. "Blind in Texas"—W.A.S.P.
41. "Gutbucket Blues"—Ghoul
42. "Booze and Hate"—Morningstar
43. "Punk and Belligerent"—Warrior Soul
44. "Drinkfightfuck"—Blood Duster
45. "Alcohol Fueled Brutality"—Debauchery
46. "Drunk Driving"—Sublime
47. "Stoned and Drunk"—Black Label Society
48. "Cirrhoetic Liver Distillation"—Haemorrhage
49. "(Empty) Tankard"—Tankard
50. "D.P.W."—Houwitser

73 Metal Bands with Druggy or Boozy Names

1. 8 Foot Sativa
2. Beer Vomit
3. Addicted
4. 26 Beers
5. T.A.Z. ("The Alcoholic Zone")
6. Drunk as Fuck
7. Beerkraft
8. Alcoholic Rites

9. Alice in Chains (According to legend, Layne Staley once said "Alice" refers to a weak or frail person, and the "Chains" are that person's addiction.)
10. Drug Honkey
11. Alcoholic Death
12. Beer Corpse
13. Alcoholocaust
14. Drunk Motherfuckers
15. Beer Mosh
16. Alcoholicoma
17. Beer Project
18. Speedball
19. Alcoholic Bastards of Hell
20. Beer Pressure
21. Angel Dust
22. Valium
23. Blue Cheer (The West Coast power trio got their name from a popular and potent type of LSD)
24. Alcoholica
25. Drunk & Stoned
26. Alcoholic D.C.
27. Boozers
28. Vodkaos
29. Brothers of Whiskey
30. Bunkdope
31. Drunk President
32. B.D.S. ("Bleeding Drunk Skulls")
33. Cannabis Corpse (They do pot-themed covers of Cannibal Corpse songs.)
34. Alcoholic Force
35. Cocaine Cowboys
36. Wine Spirit
37. DopeSick
38. Morphia
39. Drunk Earth
40. Beer Society
41. Alcohol Killer
42. Beerhead
43. M.O.D. (The band was formed by former S.O.D. vocalist Billy Milano. He says the name means "Method of Destruction," but sometimes says it stands for "Milano's On Drugs.")

44. Drunk Horse
45. Beer Wolf
46. Crack Addict
47. Alcoholic Nightmare
48. Drunken State
49. Red Wine
50. A.C.O.A. ("Adult Children of Alcoholics")
51. Hellboozer Union
52. Drugaddicted
53. Gary Churr and the Beers
54. Crackwhore
55. Alcoholic Mosh
56. Southern Whiskey Rebellion
57. Drunken Bastard
58. Red Pill
59. Motörhead (British slang for "speed freak")
60. Drunkard
61. Six Beer
62. The Reefer Hut
63. S.D.I.D. ("Still Drowning in Drugs")
64. Alcoholic Smashing War
65. Beermug
66. Terrorbeer
67. Drünkards
68. Chronic Alcoholism
69. V.S.R. ("Vratislavice Alcoholic Roar," after a brewery in the Czech Republic)
70. Drunk Junkees
71. Alcohol
72. Whiskey Hellchild
73. Cocktaillica

41 Smack-Shootin', Coke-Snortin', Hopped-Up, Tweaked-Out Metal Tunes

1. "Kickstart My Heart"—Mötley Crüe
2. "You Could Be Mine"—Guns N' Roses
3. "Crack in the Egg"—Gwar
4. "Suicide Note Pt. 1"—Pantera

5. "Hoover Street"—Rancid
6. "This Cocaine Makes Me Feel Like I'm On This Song"—System of a Down
7. "Coke'n"—Izzy Stradlin
8. "Guilty"—Nazareth
9. "Sweet Leaf"—Black Sabbath
10. "Hand of Doom"—Black Sabbath
11. "Pool Shark"—Sublime
12. "Feel Good Hit of the Summer"—Queens of the Stone Age
13. "Ozone"—Ace Frehley
14. "Snowblind"—Black Sabbath
15. "White Line Fever"—Motörhead
16. "Cure for Pain"—Morphine
17. "Kokain"—Rammstein
18. "Master of Puppets"—Metallica
19. "Journey to the Center of the Mind"—Amboy Dukes
20. "Loaded"—Primal Scream
21. "Smoke Two Joints"—Sublime
22. "Don't Step on the Grass"—Steppenwolf
23. "Hydroponic"—311
24. "Who's Got the Herb?"—311
25. "Pharmaecopia"—Mudvayne
26. "The Pusher"—Steppenwolf
27. "Dead Men Tell No Tales"—Motörhead
28. "Shedding Skin"—Pantera
29. "Suicide Messiah"—Black Label Society
30. "Dr. Feelgood"—Mötley Crüe
31. "Mr. Brownstone"—Guns N' Roses
32. "The Needle Lies"—Queensrÿche
33. "Opium of the People"—Slipknot
34. "Junkie"—Ozzy Osbourne
35. "Dope Sick Girl"—Rancid
36. "Needles"—System of a Down
37. "Addicted to Chaos"—Megadeth
38. "Wasted Time"—Skid Row
39. "Too High to Fly"—Dokken
40. "One Fix"—Dope
41. "The Burning Red"—Machine Head

Born to Be Wired: 10 Heavy Metal Drug Busts

1. Jimi Hendrix
Hendrix was arrested at Toronto International Airport in May 1969 under suspicion of carrying heroin and hash in his luggage. During the trial Hendrix testified that the drugs weren't his but had belonged to a fan, who slipped them into his baggage without his knowledge. He was acquitted.

2. Steven Adler (Guns N' Roses)
In July 2008, Adler was arrested for "creating a disturbance" after refusing to leave an unidentified man's house. Adler had been working on *Sober Living*, a recovery facility–slash–reality show spin-off named for the rehab facility where he was living after his run on *Celebrity Rehab with Dr. Drew*. Police answering the complaint arrested Adler for possession of narcotics and carried out an outstanding warrant issued after Adler missed a court appearance in 2006.

3. Sebastian Bach (Skid Row)
Bas was arrested at Middletown, New Jersey, hot spot the Lincroft Inn for "making terrorist threats" during a bar fight in which he threatened to go get a gun and shoot the bartender. Police found Bach holding five grams of weed and four packs of rolling papers. Assault charges were dropped for "lack of prosecution" after the bartender failed to show up to trial, but Bach received a sentence on the drugs: a conditional discharge, which included an $860 fine and a year's supervision.

4. David Lee Roth (Van Halen)
During his solo years, Roth was arrested in New York City's Washington Square Park trying to buy a $10 bag of what he later called "bunk" reefer from an undercover cop.

5. Bon Scott (AC/DC)
Scott earned notoriety for being in the first music group arrested in Australia for possession of marijuana, when he was a member of the bubblegum pop band the Valentines in 1969.

6. Doc McGhee (manager)
Manager to stars including Kiss, Scorpions, Mötley Crüe, and Bon Jovi, McGhee was convicted in 1987 for smuggling twenty tons of marijuana five years earlier. After

entering a guilty plea, McGhee got a five-year suspended sentence and a $15,000 fine, and, since it was his second drug trafficking offense (he'd previously been busted smuggling cocaine), was ordered to create an anti-drug foundation, leading to the establishment of the Make a Difference Foundation.

7. Jimmy Page (Led Zeppelin)
Page has been arrested for drug possession twice: In the early '80s he was taken in London, where he was trying to buy traveler's checks but couldn't produce any identification. Page himself actually told clerk to call the cops, who took him into custody when a bag of cocaine fell out of his pocket. The guitarist was given a twelve-month conditional release and a $100 fine. A 1984 tour by his band the Firm was delayed when Page was arrested in London a second time. Again he got off light, paying a $450 fine.

8. Mark St. John (Kiss)
In September 2006, ex-Kiss guitarist St. John was sent to Theo Lacy Jail in California for two weeks after pleading guilty to possession of drug paraphernalia, resisting arrest, and conspiring to destroy evidence. During his time in stir, he was given a jailhouse beat-down by a number of prisoners—with the approval of at least one prison guard—for stealing crackers from another inmate. St. John died in 2007 after a brain hemorrhage brought on by an accidental meth OD.

9. Paul Gray (Slipknot)
Gray was picked up in Des Moines, Iowa, after running a red light in his Porsche and hitting another car. After police saw him stumbling and barely coherent, they searched his car and found two hypodermic needles, cocaine, and marijuana.

10. Lemmy Kilmister (Motörhead)
While touring with space-rockers Hawkwind in 1975, Lemmy was arrested in Canada for possession of a white powder. At arrest the white powder was identified as cocaine, a drug Lemmy has always hated. The powder was actually methamphetamine, a drug Lemmy has always loved, and the misidentification led to Lemmy being set free—by both the police and Hawkwind, who sacked him from the band not long after.

RICHARD CHRISTY OF ICED EARTH AND *THE HOWARD STERN SHOW*'S TOP 5 HEAVY METAL LYRICS YOU'D MOST LIKELY HEAR REFERRED TO AT A KEG PARTY IN UNIONTOWN, KANSAS, IN 1989

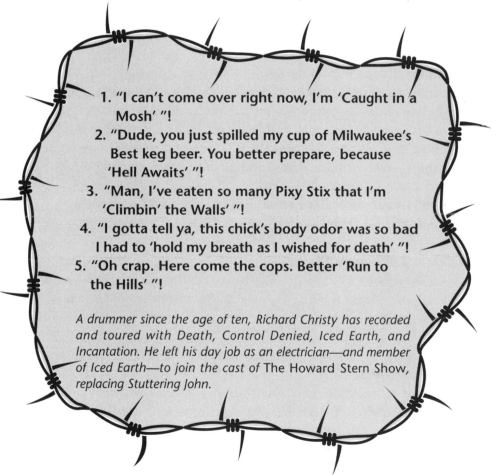

1. "I can't come over right now, I'm 'Caught in a Mosh' "!
2. "Dude, you just spilled my cup of Milwaukee's Best keg beer. You better prepare, because 'Hell Awaits' "!
3. "Man, I've eaten so many Pixy Stix that I'm 'Climbin' the Walls' "!
4. "I gotta tell ya, this chick's body odor was so bad I had to 'hold my breath as I wished for death' "!
5. "Oh crap. Here come the cops. Better 'Run to the Hills' "!

A drummer since the age of ten, Richard Christy has recorded and toured with Death, Control Denied, Iced Earth, and Incantation. He left his day job as an electrician—and member of Iced Earth—to join the cast of The Howard Stern Show, *replacing Stuttering John.*

12 Fatal Drug Overdoses and One Drug OD Who Came Back from the Dead

1. Layne Staley (Alice in Chains)
The vocalist lost a long battle with drug addiction in 2002 after doing a fatal speedball. At the time of his death, Staley, who was six foot one, weighed eighty-six pounds.

2. Laurent Bernat (Satan Jokers)
The bass player OD'd in 2004.

3. Tommy Bolin (Deep Purple)
There are two versions of Bolin's 1976 death. One claims he was found unconscious after a gig in Miami and taken to his hotel room by management to sleep it off; his health got worse and the next day his girlfriend called an ambulance, which failed to reach him in time. Another version has Bolin getting so fucked up on beer, wine, downers, cocaine, and morphine that his throat contracted, choking him to death.

4. Erik "Grim" Brødreskift (Immortal, Borknagar, and Gorgoroth)
The drummer killed himself with an overdose of pills in October 1999.

5. Steve Clark (Def Leppard)
After a long bout with alcoholism, Clark passed away at his home of what was officially called an accidental overdose in 1991. An autopsy found a massive amount of antidepressants and painkillers in his system along with three times the legal amount of alcohol.

6. Kevin DuBrow (Quiet Riot)
DuBrow died of an accidental cocaine overdose at his Las Vegas home in 2007. According to one report, he'd been dead for almost a week before his body was found.

7. Jeff "Tchort" Elrod (Masochist, Wind of the Black Mountains)
The singer/songwriter overdosed in 2006.

8. Michael Hasse (Death Attack)
The drummer of the first extreme metal band in Wolfsburg, Germany, was found dead in 1994.

9. Alexander Magoo (Mutilator, Chemako)

Circumstances surrounding his death are mysterious, but a probable OD killed Magoo in 2001.

10. Bryan Ottoson (American Head Charge)

An overdose of prescription drugs killed the guitar player in 2005. He was found in his bunk in the band's tour bus.

11. Elin Overskott (Dismal Euphony)

The keyboard player died in 2004 of a heroin overdose at the age of twenty-four.

12. Robbin Crosby (Ratt)

The success of Ratt led to depression and substance abuse for Crosby; his heroin addiction led to him being kicked out of the group in 1990. Crosby announced he was HIV-positive in 2001 and died after taking an excessively large amount of smack on June 6, 2002.

Honorable Mention

Nikki Sixx (Mötley Crüe)

Nikki has OD'd on heroin at least twice. The first time was during a post-gig drug run with Hanoi Rocks guitarist Andy McCoy. After letting McCoy shoot him up, Sixx turned blue and passed out; their dealer tried to revive him by beating him with a baseball bat before giving up and leaving him in a Dumpster. The second time was in 1987, when he was clinically dead for two minutes. He was brought back to life with two shots of adrenaline injected in his heart by a paramedic Sixx later claimed was a Crüe fan who wouldn't let him snuff it. That incident inspired the hit "Kickstart My Heart."

We Have a Drink or Two. . . Well, Maybe Three: How 11 Metalheads Knock 'Em Back

1. Alice Cooper

The Coop was drinking buddies with Jim Morrison in the late '60s and had a great fondness for Budweiser (he was seldom seen without one offstage) before eventually working his liver up to a quart of Seagram's VO a day. He drank onstage and off for years, often doing interviews and television programs as what he's called "an invisible

alcoholic," and one of his early solo albums, *From the Inside*, dealt with his (first) stint in rehab. "I was throwing up blood every morning," he recalls. "That's not a good sign at all." Now sober for twenty-seven years, he calls Diet Coke his current drink of choice.

2. Lemmy Kilmister (Motörhead)
Lemmy likes bourbon. "I drink bourbon and Coke," he says. "Any kind, as long as it says bourbon on it. I can't stand Scotch. I don't like them Canadian blend whiskeys, either. I'd rather have Jim Beam, Jack Daniel's, Wild Turkey, Maker's Mark. Maker's Mark is very good."

3. John Bonham (Led Zeppelin)
Bonzo was a fan of, among other things, Black Russians. Whisky A Go Go owner Mario Maglieri once saw Bonham down more than twenty of the Kahlúa-and-vodka cocktails at the Rainbow Bar and Grill, where Bonham became so violent he that he punched out his chauffeur and a few of the bar's customers. Maglieri had to clobber Bonham himself, giving the burly drummer thirteen stitches. Richard Cole wrote in *Stairway to Heaven* that when it came to his and Bonzo's taste in booze, "[we] weren't as fussy [as Robert Plant and John Paul Jones]. Drambuie, beer, champagne, we'd drink just about anything."

4. "Dimebag" Darrell Abbott (Pantera, Damageplan)
One of the late guitarist's favorite cocktails was a Black Tooth Grin: a shot of Seagram's and a shot of Royal Crown mixed with a splash of Coke.

5. Duff McKagan (Guns N' Roses)
Duff McKagan earned the nickname "the King of Beers" through his mighty alcohol consumption. Duff and Slash made news when accepting their second statue of the night at the American Music Awards in 1990 when, obviously plastered, they staggered to the podium and managed to also drop the F-bomb twice on live TV before having their microphone cut. McKagan gave up drinking and drugging in 1994 after his pancreas exploded.

6. Dave Mustaine (Megadeth)
Mustaine was kicked out of Metallica right before they recorded *Kill 'Em All in* 1983 in good part because of his uncontrollable behavior after he'd had too many. In one such incident, he electrocuted Ron McGovney by pouring a beer onto his bass guitar. Since getting therapy, finding God, and going off the booze, he's developed his own brand of coffee, Dave Mustaine's Blend, which he sells online.

7. James Hetfield (Metallica)

Coors Light, Pacifico, and Bombay Sapphire martinis are the choice for Hetfield. From the beginning Metallica were an alcohol-fueled group, and were shown in one of their earlier videos buying beer while they were still underage.

8. Ritchie Blackmore (Deep Purple, Rainbow)

Blackmore has a taste for the grape, preferring Wehlener Sonnenuhr, a German white, and vintage from California when it comes to red.

9. Michael Anthony (Van Halen)

Does he drink actually Jack Daniel's, or are rumors true that he swigs iced tea from that bottle he keeps onstage? Whatever. He must like it, because he had a bass shaped like a JD bottle made by Yamaha in 1984.

10. Chris Holmes (W.A.S.P.)

Holmes emptied a few bottles of vodka during his notorious interview in *The Decline of Western Civilization Part 2: The Metal Years*, director Penelope Spheeris's exposé on the sleazier side of metal. In the documentary *Heavy: The Story of Metal*, Spheeris remembers Holmes saying he didn't care where he was interviewed as long as he could drink vodka. He does just that floating in a chair in his pool, guzzling half a bottle at a time and pouring it all over himself while his mother watches.

11. Lita Ford

Chris Holmes's ex-wife had a taste for Stoli back in the day and has a guitar shaped like a bottle.

Honey 1%'er of the Cycle Sluts from Hell's 5 Best Places to Drink and Listen to Metal in New York City in the '80s

1. Lismar Lounge

This East Village dive bar was an alcohol-drenched, divine convergence of aspiring musicians, bikers, punk legends, rock stars, and eventually throngs of A&R people from near and far. If you hung out at the Lismar regularly and your band still didn't get signed, you probably really sucked.

Fave Moment: When Matt Dillon was turned away at the door for being Matt Dillon.

2. Scrap Bar

A Mecca for metalheads that actually had quite a long run for a bar of its kind. You could walk in and anyone from Slash to Lemmy would be holding up the bar.

Fave Moment: Sitting next to a girl downing pint glasses of vodka cranberry through a straw; the fact that her jaw was wired shut wasn't going to interfere at all with her good time. I said to her, "You better be careful, lady. If that comes back up, it has nowhere to go." "Nah," she said, "I do this every night." Naturally, we became lifelong friends.

3. King Tut's Wah-Wah Hut

The beer was cheap and the Jägermeister flowed freely. If you were lucky you were being served by a pseudo-famous, broke-as-hell Cycle Slut who got through the night by drinking with you. If you were unlucky you were being totally ignored.

Fun Fact: Yuppie scum were promptly ejected.

4. Alcatraz

The main attraction was my bartending Cycle Sluts from Hell bandmate, the gorgeous She-Fire of Ice, who was as easy on the eyes as she was hard on the liver. Her Kamikaze shots were no joke, and I recall members of Metallica downing 'em voraciously.

5. The Ritz

Without a doubt one of the best places to drink and see a show. You'd watch videos on the club's big screen and get shitfaced with various luminaries who might or might not outdrink you. The Ritz was a gilded art deco throwback, and the beleaguered bar staff was a bunch of stunning chicks. Most of 'em were in metal bands and each one was more pissed off than the next. Ramones, Guns N' Roses, Kiss, Motörhead, Wendy O. Williams, Manowar, and others provided the backdrop for all the melodrama, but after the show everyone was drunk and thick as thieves. Better than any miniseries HBO could ever dream up.

Fave Moment: Meeting Johnny Cash and June Carter Cash in the VIP room after their show.

Donna (a.k.a. Dava) She Wolf slings axe and fronts the band She Wolves. She's also known for writing '80s anthem "I Wish You Were a Beer" while doing time in the Cycle Sluts from Hell as Honey 1%'er. She has enjoyed the rare privilege of touring, recording, and/or performing with legends such as the Ramones, Motörhead, Sylvain Sylvain, and Jayne County, among others. She currently lives on the L.E.S. with a culinary genius and two spoiled rotten Chihuahuas.

Kittie's Top 6 "Get Drunk for Under $30" Wines

1. Haras Character (Chile)

Obviously Chile knows what they're doing when it comes to wine, and the ladies of Kittie agree. This cabernet sauvignon (2004) was our manager/dad's favorite, so we've chosen this wine as our number one in homage to him. He always knew how to entertain, and on a special night this wine would enhance the dinner and help conversation flow. Such a good wine!

2. Wolf Blass Yellow Label (Australia)

This is our go-to wine for date nights and nights out at a good restaurant. It's a great wine without being too pricey, so you can feel like you're drinking an expensive vintage without the pain to your wallet. And no hangovers!

3. Concha Y Toro Casillero del Diablo (Chile)

Any wine that has to do with Satan is cool with us. You can pretty much count on finding this wine anywhere, and since it's an award winner, you can also count on affordable quality.

4. Cono Sur (Chile)

Their cab sauv is sort of a staple for Sunday night steak dinner at Kittie HQ. Again, it's a really good, consistent wine. It only comes in huge 1.5 liter bottles to ensure that everyone has purple teeth by the end of the night.

5. Yellowtail (Australia)

The ladies of Kittie are definitely not picky when it comes to this brand of wine. From the chardonnay to the shiraz to the cab sauv, Yellowtail is cheap, consistent, and always tasty.

6. Fresita Strawberry Sparkling Wine (Chile)

We discovered this gem at a food-and-wine show. It's a strawberry-infused sparkling wine made with fresh-picked fruit from Patagonia. It's sort of like the poor man's Cristal (at least we like to think so), and has become our party drink of choice. It's not too sweet so it's very drinkable, and when you puke, it's the prettiest color of pink!

Kittie was founded in 1996 by sisters Mercedes and Morgan Lander, who were just fifteen and seventeen years old when their first CD, Split, was released. They have appeared at major European festivals such as Dynamo, Rock-Am-Ring, and Ozzfest. They've had brushes with greatness and near misses with extinction but have never surrendered.

"Saucy" Jack Bastard's 12 Drinks That'll Bang Your Head

Metal mixologist "Saucy" Jack Bastard offers recipes for a dozen drinks you can swill the next time you're rocking out. You can thank him later.

1. The Venom
A Snakebite shot with a Newcastle Brown Ale chaser
Snakebite:
1 part whiskey or bourbon
1 part gold tequila
5 drops hot sauce
Five or six of these and it's welcome to hell!

2. Sabbath Bloody Mary
3 oz. vodka or gin
8 oz. V8 or tomato juice
Dash of minced garlic or garlic paste
Dash of onion salt
Dash of black pepper
Dash of cayenne pepper
Dash of soy sauce
Dash of lime juice
Combine all ingredients in shaker with ice and shake well. Pour into highball glass filled with ice. Garnish with celery and serve with pitted black olives on a skewer. Never add Worcestershire sauce. Like Geezer Butler and Bill Ward, this drink is vegetarian.

3. Black Metal
Chase a shot of Goldschläger with a pint of your favorite porter (or stout, if porter is unavailable).

4. AC/DC
2 oz. Absolut Kurant
2 oz. crème de cassis
Combine ingredients and serve over ice.

5. Reign in Blood

3 oz. vodka

8 oz. blood orange juice

Combine in highball glass over ice. Splatter 5 or 6 drops of grenadine syrup on top.

6. Pure Fucking Armageddon

2 oz. Stroh rum

2 oz. Norwegian vodka

2 oz. black Sambuca

Mix ingredients and divide between two separate shot glasses. Set both shots on fire; allow them to burn like the very depths of hell for 10 to 15 seconds to warm. Take one in each hand, blow the shots out, and drink together.

7. British Steel

2 oz. of your favorite British gin

6 oz. Lucozade (British Red Bull)

Garnish with lime and serve over ice. Substitute vodka if desired. Do not blow brains out.

8. The Diamond Dave

2 oz. vodka

2 oz. spiced rum

2 oz. peach schnapps

4 oz. orange juice

2 oz. cranberry juice

Combine ingredients in pint glass over ice and garnish with lime. Serve with a lot of attitude.

9. Green Manalishi

2 oz. absinthe

2 oz. lemon-flavored rum

Shake over ice and strain into rocks glass rimmed with a two-prong crown of cinnamon and sugar.

10. Stryper

A shot of Heaven Hill bourbon and a Red Stripe beer chaser.

Five or six of these and you'll see God.

11. Metallitini

2 oz. silver vodka

2 oz. dry gin

1½ oz. dry vermouth

Chill two martini glasses with ice. Combine ingredients in cocktail shaker with a few ice cubes. Stir (do not shake) ingredients. Remove ice from martini glasses and wipe rim of glasses with a slice of lemon. Strain ingredients into both martini glasses and garnish with cocktail onion or olive.

12. Cocaine Cowboy

2 oz. Agwa de Bolivia coca leaf liqueur

2 oz. Jim Beam

Combine ingredients in rocks glass and hoover it down through a straw. Yee-haw!

Metal mixologist "Saucy" Jack Bastard has dedicated his life to constructing the perfect metal drink menu, with hopes of opening his own heavy metal nightclub. He spends way too much time out on the tiles.

(⊕CCUL✝)

Finally! Proof Positive That (at Least) 8 Heavy Metal Acts Indulge in Devil Worship, Drug Use, and Sexual Perversity

Hidden and Satanic Messages in Rock Music was a syndicated radio show that aired on Christian stations in 1981. Presented as an interview with Christian soldier Michael Mills, its accuses everyone from Led Zeppelin and Black Sabbath to Dan Fogelberg and Blondie of trying to warp the minds of American youth with "the rock and roll." Spouting anti-rock agitprop with a delivery worthy of Criswell, Mills exposed some of metal's biggest names as agents of the devil, using the following evidence.

1. Black Sabbath
The title of their greatest-hits package *We Sold Our Souls for Rock and Roll* and the songs "The Wizard," "Sweet Leaf," "Children of the Grave," "Fairies Wear Boots," and "Warning" prove that their master is . . . Satan!

2. AC/DC
"On the street," Mills states, "'AC/DC' stands for 'bisexual,'" which means that "it doesn't matter what kind of sex [the band] have!" The cover of *If You Want Blood* . . . shows a sacrifice like those performed in satanic rituals! *Highway to Hell* shows Angus Young with horns and a pointed tail and features the songs "Let There Be

Rock," "Highway to Hell," "Rock 'n' Roll Damnation," and "Hell Ain't a Bad Place to Be." Mills cites one of his favorite themes—the repetition of words as satanic mind control—in the song "For Those About to Rock," adding that the device is also used in Burger King ads. He then speculates about exactly what kind of venom the band sing about in "Inject the Venom" and claims that the short space of time between the end of the song "Evil Walks" and the beginning of "C.O.D." is yet another method of satanic mind control.

3. Led Zeppelin

Mills claims that the cover of *Presence* shows a woman "drawing power" from the obelisk with one hand and putting it into the mind of the boy with the other. He also points to the phrase "Words have two meanings" in "Stairway to Heaven" as a clue to the following satanic backwards message in that song: "Listen, we've been there. Because I live, serve me. There's no escaping it. Satan! If we gotta live for Satan . . . Master Satan!" Mills also says that the vocals right before the breakdown in "Stairway" sound like the biblical "wailing and gnashing of teeth." When you play them backwards, of course.

4. Lucifer's Friend

Mentions their album title, *Sneak Me In*.

5. Judas Priest

Mills talks about the songs "Hell Bent for Leather, "Evil Fantasies," "Metal Gods," "Saints in Hell," and "Beyond the Realms Of Death" from the record *Sin After Sin*.

6. Ozzy Osbourne

Mills warns the world about the *Diary of a Madman* cover. Ozzy has a "demonically painted face" and stands "in contempt of Christianity" in front of an inverted cross near a child and a strangled pigeon. His ripped pants show "some sort of symbol on his leg," which most people call "tattoos." There's also "a demonic face, somehow implanted on the whole back of the cover." Not surprisingly, no one could really see the image until he enlarged it for the lecture/slide shows he gave around the country at the time. He credits the *Diary of a Madman* slide with saving the soul of at least one member of "a Chicago rock band" who dropped to his knees and accepted Jesus as his personal savior when he saw it.

7. Kiss

The band, "sometimes referred to as 'Kings in Satanic Service,'" wear "sadomasoch-istic chains" and "demonically painted faces." Mills warns that Gene Simmons pukes blood, his "extended, serpentlike tongue" is an ancient symbol of demonic worship, and he has bragged about banging a thousand women. Mills also laments the $117 million in merch the band sells to the eight- and nine-year-olds who are the "virgin souls" Gene sings about in "God of Thunder."

8. Queen

When you play the line "Another one bites the dust" backwards, Freddie Mercury sings, "Some of us smoke marijuana."

Dr. Phibes of Blood Farmers' Evolution of Occult Metal in 13 Songs

1. "Black Sabbath" (Black Sabbath)

Bands like Coven and Black Widow were around when this was released in 1970, but they were sonic lightweights compared to Black Sabbath. This song, inspired by lyricist Geezer Butler's experience with a supernatural haunting, gave birth to true occult metal. After the Hammer horror church-bell-and-thunder intro, the band crushes those infamous three notes: the "Diabolus in Musica," outlawed as musical heresy in the Middle Ages. "Satan's coming around the bend" perfectly sums up what was in store for heavy metal once Sabbath laid down the law.

2. "7 Screaming Diz-busters" (Blue Öyster Cult)

Blue Öyster Cult weren't as scary as Sabbath, but their lyricists were successful in making fans feel they were into something mysterious. Penned by Sandy Pearlman, the band's guru and an expert on arcane lore, occult practices, and cabalistic conspiracies, this song tells of mysterious beings who summon Lucifer as the Lord of Light. The song breaks down in the middle with spooky keyboards, demented laughing, and vague descriptions of these demons who roam the night sky. When performed live, it stretched on in an improvised free-for-all where vocalist Eric Bloom would speak with Lucifer himself, calling him "Lu" to boot!

3. "In League with Satan" (Venom)

Newcastle's Venom was the first band to go completely over the top with devil worship. Their lyrics, artwork, costumes, even their names (Cronos, Mantas, and Abaddon) were 100 percent satanic. Sure, they didn't really mean the mumbo jumbo they spewed, but at the time they sounded like hell in a cement mixer. Their debut album, *Welcome to Hell*, basically invented extreme metal, and a lot of more serious-minded occult musicians got their inspiration from the first three Venom records. Hearing Cronos croak, "I kill a newborn baby/ Tear the infant's flesh" was the thrash metal litmus test in the early '80s. If you dug it, you were cool. If not, you were a poser.

4. "The Number of the Beast" (Iron Maiden)

Opening with a recitation from the Book of Revelation, this song introduced heavy metal's now obligatory reference to "666." Based on Nathaniel Hawthorne's story "Young Goodman Brown," it tells of one man's struggle with temptation as he witnesses an occult ritual in the woods. Maiden took a lot of flack for this tune at the time, probably because, unlike Venom or Mercyful Fate, they were hugely popular. In the end, though, it's just another harmless slice of Steve Harris fiction set to a galloping beat by the greatest heavy metal band since Black Sabbath.

5. "White Magic/Black Magic" (Saint Vitus)

Los Angeles's godfathers of doom metal made no bones about believing in God (they thank "The Big Man Above," right next to LSD and Budweiser in the liner notes), but for all his piety band leader Dave Chandler sure was obsessed with spirituality's dark side. Nowhere is his philosophical conflict more evident than on this track, a slow burner that describes his vacillation between good and evil. Scott Reagers moans, "Whi-i-i-te magic! Bla-a-a-ck magic!" over and over at the end, accompanied by 12-bpm drums, guitar feedback, and thunderous bass reverb. In the end, the narrator uses both styles of magic to destroy his enemies.

6. "A Dangerous Meeting" (Mercyful Fate)

Master of the macabre, real-life worshipper of Satan, and a gentleman to boot, King Diamond's been doing the Satan thing for over twenty-five years now. This track from the Fate's second album describes a midnight gathering of seven occultists who raise the dead by necromancy with dire consequences. King goes from inhuman growls to piercing high-pitched screams, and when he sings, "Some people have lost their way, some people have lost their minds/ They're gonna get themselves killed!" you get the idea he's warning of the dangers inherent when children play with dead things.

7. "Sinister" (Pentagram)

Bobby Liebling had been playing occult-tinged metal on the D.C. circuit since 1971, but it wasn't until he met up with guitarist Victor Griffin in 1982 that things got really sick. In this all-time classic doom metal track, Bobby sings Victor's first-person lyrics about an evil despot bearing a more-than-passing resemblance to Brazilian horror movie legend Coffin Joe, who has "hands of fright" and seeks a virgin to conceive his devil child! The song's title perfectly describes its music; these riffs are menacing, powerful, and deadly. Victor later became a born-again Christian and, as a solo artist, performed this song with its lyrics altered to reflect his newfound spirituality.

8. "The Exorcist" (Possessed)

Arguably the first death metal album, Possessed's *Seven Churches* is a no-holds-barred thrash assault made by precocious San Francisco teenagers obsessed with the devil. Each song is an overload of satanic imagery, violent music, and fuck-you punk attitude, the caustic vocals of Jeff Becerra making Cronos sound like Steve Perry. Heavily influenced by early Slayer but even more unhinged, Possessed took thrash up a notch and influenced a new generation to get even more extreme in the '90s. In a case of bad satanic karma, Becerra was left a paraplegic after a robbery attempt, while the only non-satanist in the group, Larry LaLonde, went on to fame and fortune in the decidedly nonthreatening Primus.

9. "Altar of Sacrifice" (Slayer)

Slayer is the one mega-successful metal band that never compromised or forgot their roots. All of their albums are outrageously satanic, and while *Show No Mercy*, *Haunting the Chapel*, and *Hell Awaits* have the most occult content, this track from the genre-defining *Reign in Blood* best displays their utter brutality. In just under three minutes Tom Araya spews out thirty-six venomous lines of human sacrifice and bloody, perverse horror. When he draws out the classic "Enter . . . to . . . the . . . realm . . . of . . . Satan!" and another chaotic, twisted guitar solo squeals off into the stratosphere, satanic nirvana is achieved.

10. "Enter the Eternal Fire" (Bathory)

If you want to lay the blame for the musical and criminal insanity of Scandinavian black metal in the early '90s on somebody, look to the late, great Quorthon of Sweden's mysterious Bathory. His first three albums were as overtly satanic as anybody's, but their sound was totally unique. Hideous production values; ghastly chain-saw guitars; raspy, incomprehensible shrieks . . . Metal fans had to be especially twisted to like this trash—and like it they did. This longer, more mature song comes on the cusp of Quorthon's transition to a Pagan-themed, epic-metal sound and describes a sinner's journey up the river Styx and eventual encounter with Satan, to whom he wholeheartedly bows down.

11. "De Mysteriis Dom Sathanas" (Mayhem)

Easily the most evil-sounding song on this list, "De Mysteriis Dom Sathanas" has all that's great about early Norwegian black metal: blasting drums, atonal but melodic guitar riffs, and frighteningly unpredictable vocals. This song describes a satanic black mass in graphic detail, from a book made of human skin to a cauldron of blood to a sacrificial goat. This is dangerous stuff, but atmospheric despite its ferocity. Shortly after this recording, Mayhem guitarist Euronymous was murdered by his own bassist in a bizarre struggle to see who was more evil. Guess Euronymous lost.

12. "Inno a Satana" (Emperor)

Black metal ne'er-do-well and teenage musical prodigy Ihsahn wrote this unabash-edly religious devotional to Satan as the final track of Emperor's influential debut album, *In the Nightside Eclipse*. The song concludes with the lines "Forever will I bleed for thee, forever will I praise Thy dreaded name / Forever will I serve thee, and Thou shalt forever prevail." It was this attitude that led Emperor and many other Norwegian bands of the early '90s to not only talk the talk but also walk the walk; by the time this was released, all the musicians on this song except Ihsahn were in prison for murder, church arson, assault, or grave desecration. After a two-year hiatus they returned to become one of the most successful—and easily the most respected—black metal bands of the '90s. They never let up on their infernal message, and they split up with class once they accomplished all they set out to do.

13. "Supercoven" (Electric Wizard)

This thirteen-minute mindfuck sums up everything great about the band's original incarnation: drugged-out sound effects; murky, distorted vocals; mystical chanting; obscenely loud bass; and a sense that Armageddon is fast approaching. Electric Wizard are deeply steeped in classic horror movie imagery from the '60s and '70s, and their songs play out like a loud Jess Franco nightmare. This song's lyrics concern a Lovecraftian cult, mindlessly enslaved to the Ancient Ones, praying for their return as a sign of the Apocalypse. Vocalist Jus Oborn's hatred of humanity may be more mired in fantasy here than in some of the Wizard's other songs, but it clearly shines through. When he's shrieking "Supercoven!" over and over at song's end, blowing out the microphone signal even after the music has ended, it's obvious he's an occult metal lifer, through and through.

Horror fanatic, obscure music collector, die-hard punk and metal-head Phil Markonish is a self-described "reader of arcane texts, veteran of the psychic and chemical wars, and seeker of the Black Arts." He was the original bassist of the Blood Farmers, playing under the name "Dr. Phibes" alongside his cousin, guitarist David Szulkin. Phil has also played in the bands Afterbirth, Hordes of Mungo, and Burning Illusions.

7 Links Between Led Zeppelin and the Occult

1. Led Zeppelin at the Crossroads
It's long been rumored that the band, with the exception of John Bonham, sold their souls to the devil in return for fame and fortune. To this day the band, with the exception of John Bonham, denies it.

2. Jimmy Page Hearts Aleister Crowley
Jimmy Page owns one of the world's largest collections of original Crowley books and memorabilia, second only to filmmaker and author Kenneth Anger. For years Page operated Equinox, a London occult bookstore that specialized in rare Crowley editions, and at one time he owned the magician's mansion Boleskine House, on the shores of Loch Ness in Scotland.

3. The *Lucifer Rising* Sound Track
Jimmy Page and Kenneth Anger met in 1973 at an auction of Crowley memorabilia, and Anger recruited the guitarist to score his film about the notorious magus. Page never finished his part of the project, but the twenty-three minutes he did compose were bootlegged after being recorded during a screening of the film as a work in progress. Its synthesized drones, ambient tones, soaring guitar lines, and eerie sound effects foreshadow Page's later sound track to *Death Wish II*, and short excerpts are said to be in the collage at the beginning of the Led Zeppelin tune "In the Evening."

4. The Kenneth Anger Curse
In 1976, Page had been letting Anger use space in his London estate as an editing bay to cut *Lucifer Rising*, but after a disagreement caused some bad blood developed between the two, Page (or his girlfriend, depending on who's telling the story) threw Anger out of the house. Anger, in response, threw Page off the film project and then threw a curse against him. Page called Anger's curse "pathetic" and nothing more than "silly little letters," but some credit those pathetic, silly little letters with the death of Robert Plant's son from a viral infection in 1977; the death of John Bonham three years later; and the death of Led Zeppelin shortly after that.

5. Zoso
The truth behind Jimmy Page's rune has never been revealed, but there are several theories about its meaning. Stephen Davis, author of Zep biography *Hammer of the*

Gods, calls the symbol a "stylized 666." The symbol also appears in a textbook for the Red Dragon Society (a secret society like Yale's Skull and Bones that makes its home at New York University) among a group of glyphs representing Saturn, the planet that rules Page's zodiac sign, Capricorn. Zoso also closely resembles the alchemical symbol for mercury. The only public comment on the matter came during Page and Plant's 1994 appearance on the *Denton* TV show in Australia. An audience member shouts out, "Jimmy, what's your symbol mean?"; Page doesn't quite hear the question so Plant replies, "Frying tonight," a catchphrase from the film *Carry On Screaming*.

6. Automatic Writing

Automatic writing, also called "trance writing," gives mediums and those who communicate with the dead the ability to write poetry or prose with sudden, otherworldly inspiration and prowess. Robert Plant has said in interviews that some of his lyrics, notably those to "Stairway to Heaven," have come to him in this way.

7. "Stairway to Heaven"

Pure evil. The lyrics beginning with "If there's bustle in your hedgerow," when played backwards, translate to: "Oh, here's to my sweet Satan / The one whose little path would make me sad / Whose power is Satan? / He'll give those with him sweet 666 / There was a little tool shed / Where he made us suffer, sad Satan." But *everybody* knows that. . . .

8 Metal Bands Who Got Their Names from Horror Movies

1. Slayer

Some fans think the band was named for the 1981 fantasy film *Dragonslayer*. Kerry King says no fucking way, but doesn't say where the name really does come from.

2. Bad Ronald

A 1974 made-for-TV movie about a troubled teen who lives in the sealed-off basement of his recently deceased mother's house and terrorizes the home's new owners.

3. Gwar

Some say "GWAR!" is the sound Godzilla makes, although singer Dave Brockie says, "It doesn't mean Gay Women Against Rape. It doesn't mean Great White Aryan

Race. It doesn't mean Gay Weird Anal Reprobates. It doesn't even mean God What an Awful Racket. It just means Gwar, which means everything, pretty much."

4. Kill Me Kate

Harvey Keitel's character Jacob Fuller says this in the movie *From Dusk Till Dawn* just before he dies.

5. Black Sabbath

The founders of heavy metal took their name from the 1963 Mario Bava horror film. It was narrated by Boris Karloff, who also appeared as a character in its third and final vignette.

6. Ministry

Vocalist Al Jourgensen named the band after the 1944 Fritz Lang thriller *Ministry of Fear*, about a man rejoining society from an insane asylum during World War II.

7. My Bloody Valentine

A 1981 slasher flick about a killer who offs couples celebrating Valentine's Day.

8. White Zombie

This 1932 zombie flick features Bela Lugosi as a Haitian witch who helps an obsessive madman turn his beloved into a zombie.

A Nasty Hobbit: 15 Metal Bands Who Got Their Names from J.R.R. Tolkien

1. Marillion (Silmarillion)

The prog metal pioneers were inspired by J.R.R. Tolkien's book of mythical tales, *The Silmarillion*.

2. Burzum

Burzum means "darkness" in Orcish, a language spoken in *The Lord of the Rings*.

3. Gorgoroth

Gorgoroth is a level of evil in Mordor, part of Middle-earth.

4. Barad-Dûr

Located in Middle-earth.

5. Cirith Ungol

The guard tower where Frodo Baggins is kept captive.

6. Isengard

The name of a fortress in Middle-earth.

7. Sauron

Sauron *is* the Lord of the Rings.

8. Nazgul

The Nazgul are nine former mortals controlled by Sauron's Rings of Power.

9. Amon Amarth

One of several names for Mount Doom, a volcano in the Mordor section of Middle-earth where Frodo can throw the One Ring to destroy it.

10. Ephel Duath

A mountain range in the southwest of Middle-earth.

11. Morgoth

This character from *The Silmarillion* is the main source of evil in Middle-earth.

12. Galadriel

A female elf who appears in *The Lord of the Rings*, *The Silmarillion*, and *Unfinished Tales*.

13. Gandalf

A wizard who heads the Istari and is a leader among the Fellowship of the Ring.

14. Fellowship of the Ring

Group in Middle-earth who protect Frodo Baggins and the One Ring.

15. Rivendell

An outpost for elves in Middle-earth.

Body Piercing Saved My Life Author Andrew Beaujon's List of 9 Christian Metal Band Names, Translated

1. P.O.D.
The band's name stands for "Payable on Death," the idea being less that one has to answer for one's sins than that Jesus Christ's promise of salvation comes due when one slips this mortal coil.

2. Demon Hunter
They may be rocking you with their giant bald heads, big drum sets, and complicated facial hair, but in their hearts they're off in the woods, holding snarling dogs of righteousness on long leather leashes and visiting God's vengeance on evil spirits. Also, they're from Seattle.

3. As I Lay Dying
Faulkner, dude! It's the title of his 1930 novel, by way of Homer's *Odyssey*.

4. Stryper
Comes from King James Version translation of Isaiah 53:5: "And with his stripes we are healed." Other, arguably better Bible translations render the word *stripes* as *bruises* or *wounds*. Drummer Robert Sweet later determined that the band's name could be constructed as a clunky acronym: Salvation Through Redemption, Yielding Peace, Encouragement, and Righteousness, an especially impressive feat for a someone unaided by pot.

5. The Crucified
Duh.

6. Vomitorial Corpulence
You throw up a lot because you're so fat?

7. Aletheian
It's Greek, by way of Lebanon, Pennsylvania, for "truth."

8. King's X
This one's disputed. Some believe it refers to Jesus's cross, but others say it's a reference to a royal seal that could not be broken.

9. Zao

Purportedly comes from the Greek for "alive." A guy of Greek descent in my office says the Greek word for "alive" is *zoe*, but adds he doesn't know how to conjugate his parents' language and that the "zao" theory seems plausible. When an interviewer claimed the name was Latin, former vocalist Dan Weyandt said, "It doesn't necessarily mean 'alive' but spiritually alive, like having your third eye open in the sense of spiritual views." You know what? Maybe the name isn't important.

Andrew Beaujon is the managing editor of the Washington City Paper. *He has written about music for the* Washington Post, Spin, *and the* New York Times. *His 2006 book about Christian rock and evangelical Christian culture,* Body Piercing Saved My Life, *is often offered at a deep discount.*

A Kiss Is Just a Kiss: The Supposedly Evil Meanings of 3 Metal Bands' Names

The great rock wars of the '80s led fundamentalist Christians, conservative Republicans, and the ideologically confused Democrats of the PMRC to charge heavy metal bands with backward masking, subliminal seduction, and the even more unlikely idea that they were slipping subtle clues into their names to draw fans over to the dark side. Because heavy metal is so subtle . . .

1. AC/DC

Anti-Christ/Devil Child
Anti-Christ/Devil Children
Anti-Christ/Death [to] Christ
After Christ/Devil Comes
After Christ/Devil Conquered
Away [from] Christ/[the] Devil Comes

2. Kiss

Kids In Satan's Service
Kings In Satan's Service
Knights In Satan's Service
Knights In the Service of Satan

3. W.A.S.P.

We Are Sexual Perverts

THE NAMES OF 10 OF ALICE COOPER'S SNAKES

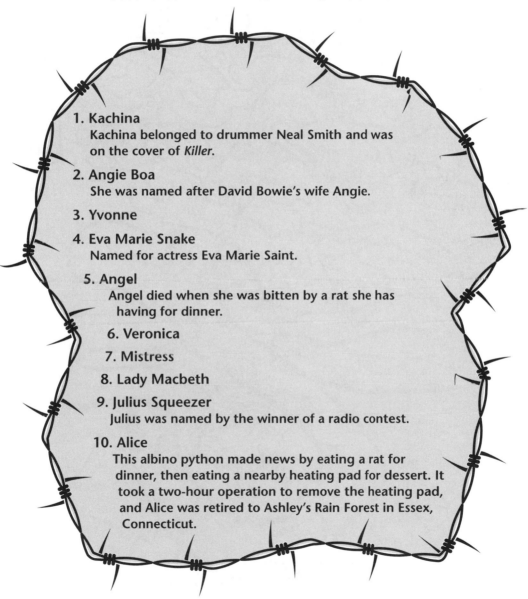

1. **Kachina**
   Kachina belonged to drummer Neal Smith and was on the cover of *Killer*.

2. **Angie Boa**
   She was named after David Bowie's wife Angie.

3. **Yvonne**

4. **Eva Marie Snake**
   Named for actress Eva Marie Saint.

5. **Angel**
   Angel died when she was bitten by a rat she has having for dinner.

6. **Veronica**

7. **Mistress**

8. **Lady Macbeth**

9. **Julius Squeezer**
   Julius was named by the winner of a radio contest.

10. **Alice**
    This albino python made news by eating a rat for dinner, then eating a nearby heating pad for dessert. It took a two-hour operation to remove the heating pad, and Alice was retired to Ashley's Rain Forest in Essex, Connecticut.

Shabbos Bloody Shabbos: 37 Headbangin' Jews

1. Scott Ian (Anthrax)
2. Dan Spitz (Anthrax)
3. Dave Spitz (Anthrax)
4. Sharon Osbourne
5. Brad Delson (Linkin Park)
6. Gene Simmons (Kiss)
7. Paul Stanley (Kiss)
8. Bruce Kulick (Kiss)
9. Eric Singer (Kiss)
10. John Silvers (Type O Negative)
11. Chris Adler (Lamb of God)
12. Vince Neil (Mötley Crüe)
13. Kerry King (Slayer)
14. Geddy Lee (Rush)
15. Brad Wilk (Rage Against the Machine)
16. Donald Roeser (Blue Öyster Cult)
17. Eric Bloom (Blue Öyster Cult)
18. Alex Skolnick (Testament)
19. Danny Lilker (Nuclear Assault)
20. Evan Seinfeld (Biohazard)
21. Danny Schuler (Biohazard)
22. Riki Rachtman (host, *Headbangers Ball*)
23. David Lee Roth (Van Halen)
24. Ross the Boss (Manowar)
25. Rick Rubin (producer)
26. Jay Jay French (Twisted Sister)
27. David Bryan (Bon Jovi)
28. Joey Kramer (Aerosmith)
29. Slash (Guns N' Roses)
30. Steven Adler (Guns N' Roses)
31. Mercedes Lander (Kittie)
32. Morgan Lander (Kittie)
33. Mike Portnoy (Dream Theater)
34. Dave Mustaine (Megadeth)
35. Marty Friedman (Megadeth)
36. David Draiman (Disturbed)
37. Rob Bourdon (Linkin Park)

Back in Unblack: 33 Christian Rock Bands Who Shout at the Devil

Not all metal bands sing hymns to Satan. Unblack metal bands do just the opposite, singing paeans to the destruction of the fallen angel.

1. Tempest
2. Horde
3. Daemonicide
4. Vomitous Discharge
5. Golgotha
6. Fire Throne
7. Poems of Shadows
8. Angel 7
9. Nordic Wolves
10. Dark Procession
11. Immortal Souls
12. Admonish
13. Wrathful Plague
14. Eternal Mystery
15. Divine Symphony
16. 3:16
17. Elgibbor
18. Zacai
19. Eternal Faith
20. Holy Blood
21. Sylvan Fortress
22. Frost Like Ashes
23. Lengsel
24. Drottnar
25. Kekal
26. Crimson Moonlight
27. Antestor
28. Fearscape
29. Shadows of Paragon
30. Ceremonial Sacred
31. Occult Mourn
32. By His Blood
33. Extol

Spinal Tap Meets *The Mummy*: Mike McPadden's 13 Favorite, Absolutely Killer Heavy Metal Horror Movies . . .

1. *Black Roses* (1988)

Beware Black Roses. The titular power-chorded combo may appear to be on-the-mascara-accurate embodiments of the hair metal moment as they gear up for a world tour, but in fact these spandexed spellbinders are bona fide demons in disguise. The group's rockin' aim is to brainwash small-town youth into eternal devotion to metal's dark arts via guitar solos, groupies, and a killer tour bus to hell (quite literally). One local PTA goes all PMRC in fear of what Black Roses might be up to with their lipstick, libidinous gyrations, and satanic lyrics. Among the worried is *The Sopranos'*

Vincent Pastore (Big Pussy!), who gets sucked into a stereo speaker that's got a taste for Italian. Such is the power of true metal.

2. *The Dungeonmaster* (1985)

In *The Dungeonmaster*, noted heavy metal icon Satan makes off with a computer geek's girlfriend and issues a decree: To win her back, our hero must overcome a series of challenges with metallic seasoning: zombies, frozen historical figures, a serial killer, a cave-dwelling troll, and high-octane pursuit across a post-nuke wasteland. And then there is the most horns-in-the-air gauntlet of all: a full-blown W.A.S.P. concert where shackled Gwen serves as the centerpiece of the stage show while Blackie Lawless and the boys wail "Tormentor." Seven different directors labored on *The Dungeonmaster*. Seven was obviously the right number for this feast.

3. *Hard Rock Zombies* (1985)

Nazi Germany and heavy metal are two monumental wellsprings of bad taste that often make great bad taste together; e.g., Slayer's "Angel of Death," the book-burning clips on MTV's *Headbangers Ball,* and of course *Hard Rock Zombies.* At a stop in a town called Grand Guignol—where Adolf Hitler still lives—a touring metal band's front man flips for a lass who sports 1974 pubic mounds where her eyebrows should be. The rocker's relentless pursuit of this hirsute honey gets his fellow musicians mixed up with the living dead of the title, along with inbred rednecks, a werewolf grandma, and homicidal dwarves (actual little people, not the guys who put out *Blood, Guts & Pussy*). And we mentioned that Hitler's in this too, right?

4. *Kiss Meets the Phantom* (1978)

Debuting on NBC with Gene, Paul, Ace, and Peter cruising around a lit-up amusement park in flying bumper cars to "Rock and Roll All Night," *Kiss Meets the Phantom* immediately blazed a before-and-after trail in pop (metal) culture. For here is where Gene Simmons breathes fire like Godzilla, Paul Stanley shoots laser beams from his eye, and a mad scientist builds Kiss look-alike robots that the real Kiss must battle with supernatural powers. It's also where Ace Frehley walked out and got replaced by an African-American actor in trademark "Space Ace" facial markings, which nobody (on-screen) notices. For years, *Kiss Meets the Phantom* was available in chintzy VHS form as *Kiss Meets the Phantom of the Park.* Throughout the '90s, it was a sought-after bootleg until finally receiving an official DVD release as *Kiss in Attack of the Phantoms.* But the TV version, as well as the longer one that lucky Europeans got to pay for in theaters, was titled *Kiss Meets the Phantom.* Accept no substitutes . . . except, of course, for that black dude in the Ace Frehley makeup.

5. *Rock 'n' Roll Nightmare* (1987)

Muscle-pumped New York rocker Jon Mikl Thor made a name for himself onstage by bending steel bars and performing other superhuman feats of strength and rockingness. In his big-screen debut, *Rock 'n' Roll Nightmare*, Thor packs the same sideshow bravado into his role as the leader of metal titans the Tritons, who steal off to a secluded farmhouse to record their next album. What the Tritons don't know is that they've stumbled upon a dwelling of ancient evil, which takes to offing group members and groupies alike, before manifesting itself as bloodthirsty foam-rubber puppets. Think those buggers could be a match for Thor? Think again. Mightily.

6. *Queen of the Damned* (2002)

After a century-long nap, vampire Lestat (Stuart Townsend) hops out of his coffin in Hollywood, stumbles upon the pulsating-with-hotties goth-metal scene, and quickly ascends to axe-hammering musical superstardom. So goes the setup to the adaptation of the Anne Rice novel *Queen of the Damned*. Complications arise when Lestat's guitar shredding awakens Akasha, Queen of All Vampires (Aaliyah). She wants the new metal god to serve as her eternal king. Alas, Lestat digs rock 'n' roll's groupies and the glory. So somebody's going to get staked where it hurts.

7. *Rocktober Blood* (1984)

Rocktober Blood arises from the time between Judas Priest getting blamed for shotgun suicides and Marilyn Manson taking heat for high school massacres. Here, heavy metal not only inspires Billy Eye (Tray Loren), vocalist for Rocktober Blood, to slaughter his own band members, but to kill a grand total of "twenty-five rock 'n' rollers" in all. Billy gets the electric chair, and his backup singer (Donna Scoggins)—who survived the rampage by stripping nude and hiding between hot tub bubbles—subsequently gets famous with theatrical metal combo Headmistress. Then, a year after frying, someone suspiciously reminiscent of Billy pops up to knock off a fresh crop of headbangers. Come to Rocktober Blood for the Alice Cooper makeup and proto-Gwar theatrics. Stay for the naked broads and gory violence. Or vice versa. It works either way.

8. *Scream Dream* (1989)

The spiky spooker *Scream Dream* chronicles the ups and downs of devil-worshipping diva Michelle Shock (Carol Carr), who ranks high among heavy metal's hottest vocalists until her dopey boyfriend kills her. It's a bummer, but Michelle's big-haired bandmates decide to carry on with the fresh pipes of Jamie Summers (Playboy honey Melissa Anne Moore). All is rocking until the new chick becomes possessed by

Michelle's malevolent spirit, causing buxom blonde Jamie to hulk out into a hell-raising demon at the slightest provocation. Filmmaker Donald Farmer pumped out *Scream Dream* smack between *Cannibal Hookers* (1987) and *Vampire Cop* (1990). Talk about the right visionary at the right time

9. *Shock 'Em Dead* (1991)

Jailbait porn phenom Traci Lords headlines *Shock 'Em Dead* as the manager of a hard rock outfit for which nerdy Martin (Stephen Quadros) auditions to be lead guitarist. He doesn't get the gig, but our boy does get a black-magic boost from the bluntly monikered Voodoo Woman (Tyger Sodipe). In short order, Martin's rocking Traci's panties off (not on camera, unfortunately) as a guitar god named Angel. Alas, there is hell to pay, literally, as Voodoo Woman rigged the deal. To stay atop the charts, Angel must consume human souls. None of this leads to Traci naked, so what price fame? Too high, indeed.

10. *Terror on Tour* (1980)

Circus-faced metallians the Clowns (played behind-the-greasepaint by true-life outfit the Names) headline *Terror on Tour*. Things are really happening for these Clowns—their Ace-Frehley-fied riffs are topping the charts, the titular roadshow is packing in crowds, and the groupies are coming fast, hard, and in the nude. Unfortunately, somebody takes to icing the Clowns' oft-topless female fans and a full-blooded, neon-Afro-wigged murder mystery ensues. Whodunnit? Director Don Edmonds, that's who, here making his second-most noteworthy (and maybe even second-most metal) contribution to cinema after his 1974 Götterdämmerung, *Ilsa, She Wolf of the SS*.

11. *Trick or Treat* (1986)

Ozzy Osbourne as a televangelist! Gene Simmons as a metal DJ named Nuke! Sound track by Fastway! Skippy from *Family Ties* as our headbanging hero who beats the bullies by invoking demons via backward-masked messages on rock records! Directed by Toad from *American Graffiti*! Such a wicked brew alas proves less alchemical than the sum of its ingredients in *Trick or Treat*, which gets its metallic surface aspects but misses the mark on attitude and core necessities such as sex and violence. We see one set of boobs and absolutely no blood. And Skippy shows his ass.

12. *Turbulence 3: Heavy Metal* (2001)

Satanic terrorism rules—almost—in *Turbulence 3: Heavy Metal*. Shock rocker Slade Craven (John Mann) is scheduled to perform a concert onboard an in-flight 747 that will be webcast worldwide, only to be kidnapped and replaced by his demon-worshipping look-alike Simon Flanders. Flanders, you see, heads up the cult Guardians of the Gateway, and he believes that a jet crash in the right spot could unleash the Embodiment of All Evil himself upon the earth. And his projected wellspring of such fertile godlessness? Eastern Kansas. We'll buy that.

13. *Musical Mutiny* (1970)

Exploitation legend Barry Mahon built his Florida-based movie empire through charmingly cracked screen-fillers aimed at the very young (*Santa and the Ice Cream Bunny*) and the ostensibly mature (*Fanny Hill Meets Dr. Erotico*). Then, at the height of long-haired freak-out mania, Mahon attempted to tap into the acid rock contingent with *Musical Mutiny*. A hippie swashbuckler emerges from the sea and bewitches all the teenagers within earshot to join him in mounting a "musical mutiny" against society. Ground zero for this rockin' revolution is Pirate's World, a local amusement park, and the marching anthems come courtesy of proto-metal pioneers Iron Butterfly.

. . . and 12 Headbanging Cameos in Non-Horror Movies

1. AC/DC in *Private Parts* (1997)

The electric thunder from down under rocks at a victory concert for star Howard Stern. *Private Parts* is not horror, as Stern has since described this cinematic valentine to the wife he divorced not long after its release as "science fiction."

2. Alice Cooper in *Sextette* (1978)

Mae West's swan song also showcases Keith Moon and Ringo Starr, but Alice gets to belt out a disco number as a piano-playing bellboy. In case his short-hair wig obscures his identity, Dom Deluise hilariously happens by on-screen and says, "Hi, Alice."

3. Axl Rose in *The Dead Pool* (1988)

The final Dirty Harry blowout includes death among the L.A. glam metal set. Look for Axl as a late-night Sunset Strip dweller in mourning.

4. Cannibal Corpse in *Ace Ventura, Pet Detective* (1994)

Family-friendly funnyman Jimmy Carrey claimed to be a big fan, then proved it to the Buffalo death-metallians by grunting out the lyrics to his favorite CC songs.

5. Dave Lombardo (Slayer) and Steve Tucker (Morbid Angel) in *Cremaster 2* (1999)

Highbrow visual artist Matthew Barney's nonsensical *Cremaster* movies include loads of unexpected guest appearances. Here, Lombardo and Tucker get to jam while scoring a costarring credit with Norman Mailer.

6. Helmet in *Jerky Boys: The Movie* (1995)

Following the flop of their second album after a famously lucrative post-Nirvana cash-in, the Manhattan alt-metal monsters ride the lightning in a rock club while the titular prank callers from Queens elude comical mobsters.

7. Jani Lane in *High Strung* (1991)

He saw red, he swallowed cherry pie, and then Warrant front man Jani Lane found his way into this bizarre ego trip written by and starring the future director of *Kung Pow: Enter the Fist.*

8. Marilyn Manson in *Jawbreaker* (1999)

Rose McGowan stars in this largely disliked teenage murder comedy. At the time, she was en route to becoming Mrs. Manson. Perhaps the shock rocker's wordless cameo as a bar sleaze who bangs the dead chick did them in as a couple.

9. Perry Farrell in *The Doom Generation* (1995)

Jane's Addiction founder Farrell is a natural fit in the cinematic world of Greg Araki, the reigning indie iconoclast of 1990s Los Angeles. Again, Rose McGowan stars. Coincidence? Yes.

10. Rob Halford in *Spun* (2002)

Hell-bent-for-leather Halford makes a perfectly convincing porn store clerk who services meth-wrecked horndogs Mickey Rourke and Jason Schwartzman.

11. Scott Ian in *Calendar Girls* (2003)

What would a brassy comedy about older British mums posing nude for charity be without a cameo by Anthrax madman Scott Ian? Well, it wouldn't be *Calendar Girls.*

12. Twisted Sister in *Pee-Wee's Big Adventure* (1995)

During Pee-Wee's climactic bicycle chase through the Warner Brothers lot, he pedals through Dee Snider and his Long Island longhairs filming a music video for "Burn in Hell." Twisted Sister's appearance, like the whole rest of the *Big Adventure*, is pure heaven.

Mike McPadden, under the pen(is) name Selwyn Harris, published the apocalyptic sleaze zine Happyland *and has toiled for Larry Flynt Publications. Other McOutlets include* The New York Press *and Peter Bagge's* HATE. *McPadden presently serves as editorial director at* Mr. Skin *and slays guitar with crotch rockers Gays in the Military. He believes the Butthole Surfers are metal, and hopes the public will someday demand a special edition DVD of his R-rated screenwriting triumph,* Animal Instincts 3: The Seductress *(1995).*

Pure Fucking Armageddon: The Norwegian Black Metal Body Count

The early-'90s Norwegian black metal scene is as notorious for the violence that surrounded it as the metal that served as its sound track. These are some of the people who sold their souls for rock 'n' roll, and those they took with them.

1. Dead (Mayhem)

In April 1991, Mayhem vocalist Dead killed himself with a shotgun. The depressed twenty-two-year-old's stage moves included slicing himself with a hunting knife and huffing the stank of a dead raven he carried in a jar while he sang. His body was found by Mayhem guitarist Euronymous, who went out and bought a camera to photograph the death scene before calling the police. Euronymous also reportedly ate some of Dead's brains and had shards of his skull made into necklaces for friends (Euronymous later denied the former but admitted the latter). Dead's story was mirrored in an episode of the TV show *Six Feet Under* when some goth kids wore the cremains of their friend in necklaces before snorting them.

2. Norwegian Churches

In the early '90s, between fifty and seventy Norwegian churches were burned in an anti-Christianity campaign carried out by members or followers of a small, intense black metal clique called the Black Circle, whose various philosophies included satanism, paganism, fascism, extreme nationalism, and racism. Varg "Count Grishnackh" Vikernes of the band Burzum was convicted of torching Fantoft Stave Church in Bergen, the first and most notorious of the arsons, and along with Jørn

Inge Tunsberg was found guilty of burning down that town's Åsane Church. Other churches set ablaze include the Storetveit Church (also in Bergen); Oslo's Hauketo Church and Holmenkollen Chapel; and the Skjold Church in Vindafjord.

3. Magne Andreassen

The day before he helped Vikernes and Euronymous burn down the Holmenkollen Chapel in August 1992, Emperor's drummer Bard "Faust" Eithun stabbed to death Magne Andreassen, a gay man Eithun claimed had propositioned him on his way home from a bar in Lillehammer. Eithun called the killing spontaneous, but bandmate Ihsahn said Eithun was obsessed with serial killers and wanted to see what it was like to murder someone. Faust later said of the killing, "There's no remorse. I took his life and I paid for it. It's not a big deal." After serving nine and a half years of a fourteen-year sentence, he was released from prison in 2003.

4. Euronymous (Øystein Aarseth)

Varg Vikernes's involvement in the Black Circle church arsons wasn't discovered until he killed Black Circle ringleader and former bandmate Euronymous in 1993 (Vikernes had briefly played bass with Mayhem). Euronymous owned the Helvete record store where the Black Circle congregated and ran the label Deathlike Silence Productions, distributor of Vikernes's own band, Burzum. Vikernes claimed that he and his accomplice Snorre Ruch went to Euronymous's apartment intending to discuss a contract, despite the fact that Vikernes had heard Euronymous was planning to kidnap him and kill him on videotape. Euronymous opened his door, saw Vikernes, and ran; Vikernes thought he was going for a knife, so he pulled out his own blade and stabbed Euronymous twenty-three times—eleven of the wounds were in the back. In 1994 he was sentenced to twenty-one years in prison.

5. Sandro Beyer

In April 1993, Andreas Kirchner, Hendrik Möbus, and Sebastian Schauseil of the band Absurd tortured and killed fifteen-year-old fellow student Sandro Beyer. Beyer was a hanger-on in the Absurd clique whom the band never really liked; after being shunned by Möbus and Schauseil, Beyer threatened to reveal Schauseil's affair with a local married woman. The trio lured Beyer to an isolated cottage where Kirchner and Schauseil strangled him while Möbus stabbed him. When it was all over, Kirchner reportedly said, "Oh shit. I've completely fucked up my life."

V
(VIOLENCE)

Peter Grant's Greatest Hits: 7 People Assaulted by the Manager of Led Zeppelin (and One Very Honorable Mention)

1. Crooked Promoters
Grant was one of a handful of promoters to import American rockers such as Chuck Berry and the Everly Brothers to tour England in the early '60s. In one of the earliest stories surrounding Grant's notorious management techniques, he's said to have beaten up a concert promoter who tried to rip off Little Richard, who was his client at the time. Grant reportedly then beat up the six cops who showed up at the scene.

2. Bootleggers
Peter Grant saw some enterprising folks videotaping the band at the 1970 Bath Festival and threw a bucket of water on them, blowing their rig up.

3. Bootleg Dealers
An unfortunate bootleg record dealer found out the hard way not to fuck with Peter Grant. The former wrestler and bouncer went to a record store posing as a customer hunting for Led Zeppelin bootlegs. When the owner said that yes, he did sell the

illicit recordings, Grant grabbed hold of him so hard he broke his forearm and said he would like to have all the bootlegs. Now.

4. More Bootleggers

If there was one thing Peter Grant hated more than people who sold bootlegs, it was people who recorded them. During Zep's 1970 gig in Vancouver, Canada, Grant saw a man down front wearing a set of headphones and pointing a microphone towards the stage. Grant demolished the microphone and what he thought was the tape recorder it was plugged into. The gear didn't belong to a bootlegger but to a representative from Canada's Noise Abatement Society, who was there to monitor sound levels of the show.

5. Wise-Ass Sailors

A couple of unfortunate swabbies spotted Jimmy Page and Jeff Beck (or Robert Plant, in some versions of the story) in an airport (or train station) in New Orleans (or Miami) and started making comments about their long, rock-star hair. Grant went over to one sailor, lifted him off the ground by his lapels and asked, "What's yer fucking problem, Popeye?" The other ran away.

6. Stupid Security Guards

The most famous incident involving Grant was the assault on Oakland Coliseum security guard Jim Matzorkis in 1977. Grant's son Warren had either asked for—or tried to steal—a wooden plaque from one of the Led Zeppelin dressing rooms. John Bonham, who had just stepped offstage, apparently saw Matzorkis slap Warren upside the head and promptly kicked Matzorkis in the balls. When Grant found out what had happened, he and an associate kicked Matzorkis' ass in a dressing room while tour manager Richard Cole stood guard outside. Two days later the four were arrested and ultimately given suspended sentences and a period of probation.

7. Still More Bootleggers

A former light man for the group tells the story of walking into a room backstage at Madison Square Garden and seeing a bootlegger being sat upon by the 300-pound-plus Grant while Led Zep road manager Richard Cole stomped him.

Very Honorable Mention

After Grant and crew demolished a Seattle hotel room, the pissed-off desk clerk said, "Yeah, I wish I could trash a hotel room and just get off by paying for the damages." Grant gave him $5,000 in cash and said, "Here. Have one on me." He did.

11 Heavy Metal Gigs That Ended in Riots (and Only 4 Were Guns N' Roses!)

1. Led Zeppelin—Vigorelli Cycling Stadium, Milan, Italy; July 5, 1971

Spurred on by unruly fans wanting free admission, political muckrackers leafleting for an upcoming demonstration, and people just digging the sounds that Zep laid down, an estimated battalion of two thousand policemen escalated a series of otherwise minor skirmishes into a full-scale riot. After several pleas by Robert Plant to stop burning things in the audience, the band realized that where there was smoke, there wasn't necessarily fire. Jimmy Page recalls, "We were playing in a cloud of tear gas but it was hopeless, so we said, 'Blow this, let's cut it really short.' We did one more number and went right in to 'Whole Lotta Love' and the whole crowd jumped up. By this point there'd been about forty minutes of tear gas attacks and finally somebody heaved a bottle at the police. It was not entirely unexpected since the crowd had been getting bombarded for no reason, but . . . that's what the police had been waiting for." By the end of the melee, roadies trying to protect Zep's gear were hospitalized, the band had hidden in the dressing room for an hour, forty people had been injured, and sixteen were arrested.

2. Led Zeppelin—Orange Bowl, Tampa, Florida; June 3, 1977

After watching guitarist Les Harvey of Stone the Crows die onstage after touching an ungrounded microphone, manager Peter Grant decided no client of his would risk electrocution again and made all Led Zeppelin gigs "no rain" affairs. So when he found out—while flying to the stadium through a storm—that a promoter has advertised Zep's Tampa show as "rain or shine" he freaked, but decided to see how things went. Things went badly: A few songs into the set it started to pour and Grant pulled the band offstage, canceling the show when the rain still hadn't stopped forty-five minutes later. According to a Tampa police spokesman, three to four thousand fans were being "unruly and disorderly," requiring 250 club-swinging policemen in riot gear to get the situation under control. By the end, more than a hundred fans and a dozen police were injured and eight fans were arrested. It was a perfect example of lightning striking twice; when tickets for this show went on sale—and quickly sold out—rampaging fans broke into the stadium and started ripping up seats and burning concession stands. A SWAT team managed to calm things down then too, thanks again to some well-applied tear gas. Similar ticket riots took place in Oklahoma City and Houston during this tour.

3. Black Sabbath—Mecca Arena, Milwaukee, Wisconsin; October 9, 1980

Three songs into their show, bassist Geezer Butler got hit in the head with a bottle, and new lead singer Ronnie James Dio scolded the crowd: "The stage is not a trash can, and we don't appreciate things being thrown at us. You've thrown something for the last time. You've hit Geezer on the head, and we don't appreciate that either. We wanted to give a lot for you, but not our blood. If you don't enjoy it, tough shit." The band walked offstage and the production manager announced that Black Sabbath wouldn't be coming back. After chanting, "Fuck you!" the crowd started to wreck the joint, throwing bottles, breaking chairs, trying to set them on fire (unsuccessfully), knocking over garbage cans, and breaking doors and railings. The band didn't return to Milwaukee for over a decade.

4. Guns N' Roses—Riverport Amphitheater, Maryland Heights, Missouri; July 2, 1991

Everything was going fine at this *Use Your Illusion* tour show until Axl saw someone in the crowd with a video camera and dove headfirst off the stage after them. He got back onstage, threw the mic down, and hit the bricks; then the crowd trashed the joint. About twenty minutes of the carnage was captured on video and released as the bootleg DVD *Riot Show*. Axl was arrested the following year and charged with four counts of assault and one count of destruction of property. He was convicted, given two years' probation, and fined $50,000.

5. Guns N' Roses—Olympic Stadium, Montreal, Canada; August 8, 1992

James Hetfield of Metallica, who were sharing co-headlining status with GNR, received second-degree burns from a pyrotechnics explosion, ending the Metallica part of the show for the evening. Despite having the chance to take the stage and save the day, Guns N' Roses couldn't go on because Axl hadn't arrived at the arena. The riot started a little over an hour into Guns N' Roses' already delayed performance, when a pissed-off Axl left the stage claiming throat problems and didn't come back. Fans trashed the stadium, then took it outside, where they broke windows, burned cars, looted stores, and set a series of fires.

6. Guns N' Roses—General Motors Place, Vancouver, Canada; November 7, 2002

Axl doesn't even have to be there to start a riot. The opening date of the Gunners' first North American tour in almost a decade was set to start at nine-thirty but was canceled at eight when promoters realized that Axl's plane, which had been delayed from Los Angeles due to mechanical problems, hadn't arrived; the rest of the band were already backstage. After being told that the show wouldn't go on, pissed-off fans hurled metal barricades through a glass door and followed up with a barrage of rocks and bottles. Cops with attack dogs soon arrived and pepper-sprayed the crowd, some of whom were also clubbed, chased, and beaten (at least one fan had his teeth knocked out). A Vancouver police spokeswoman called the police reaction "a proper show of force."

7. Guns N' Roses—First Union Center, Philadelphia, Pennsylvania; December 6, 2002

A riot started a month later when Axl again failed to show up. Clear Channel, who were sponsoring the tour, decided to cut their losses and canceled the remaining gigs.

8. System of a Down—Schrader Boulevard parking lot, Los Angeles, California; September 3, 2001

System of a Down planned a free show to thank fans the day before the release of their record *Toxicity*, only to have local fire marshals cancel it when ten thousand people turned up. Worried that the crowd would, well, riot, the fire marshals never actually told anybody that the concert was off, instead hoping the presence of riot cops on horseback would send the message. It did. The crowd rioted, bum-rushing the stage and stealing equipment. Six people were arrested and several more were injured. Vocalist Serj Tankian later blamed the Los Angeles Police Department for the disruption, saying the were "not prepared adequately for such a show of heads" and calling the aborted gig "one more blow to our freedom to convene." The LAPD blamed the promoters, saying, "It was a poorly planned event."

9. AC/DC—Monsters of Rock, Moscow, Russia; September 28, 1991

An increasingly agitated security force made up of former Soviet Army soldiers decided that the best way to handle excited fans at this Monsters of Rock show was by beating them with truncheons and water cannons.

10. Mötley Crüe—Greensboro Coliseum, Greensboro, North Carolina; October 28, 1997

In a lawsuit seeking $75,000 in damages, African-American security guard John Allen accused the band of verbal assault, battery, and infliction of emotional distress after what he claimed was a racially tinged incident. Allen claimed that Tommy Lee and Nikki Sixx used racial slurs against him—and encouraged his assault by the crowd—at the end of this gig, where the band thought Allen had been roughing up audience members. Allen also accused Lee of adding injury to insult by pouring a beer on his head as he left the stage. Nikki Sixx and Tommy Lee each received a thirty-day suspended sentence for inciting a riot and assaulting a security guard and paid about $150 in court costs. Charges of inciting a riot with ethnic intimidation were dropped.

11. Mötley Crüe—America West Arena, Phoenix, Arizona; December 10, 1997
The show ended in a riot when Vince Neil dove into the crowd after someone threw a plastic cup at him. Neil, Tommy Lee, and Nikki Sixx were all arrested and charged with assault for jumping on some cops.

51 Awesomely Violent Band Names

1. Total Fucking Destruction
2. Carcass Grinder
3. I Shit on Your Face
4. A Vulperidysictic Bio-Fest
5. Biomechanical Jigsaw Morgue
6. Die Pigeon Die
7. Inbreeding Sick
8. Carnival of Carnage
9. Bisected
10. Dismember
11. Entrails Massacre
12. Incinerate
13. Coregoremorecybershit
14. Cattle Decapitation
15. Kindergarten Hazing Ritual
16. Devourment
17. Preschool Tea Party Massacre
18. Repulsive Excremental Crypt
19. Combatwoundedveteran
20. Arsonist
21. Execution
22. Mangled Atrocity
23. Devoured Decapitation
24. Extreme Noise Terror
25. Bodies Lay Broken
26. Necrokillgraveterror
27. Fleshgore
28. Gored
29. Goretrade
30. Inducing Terror
31. Ultimo Mondo Cannibale
32. Sarcophaga Carnaria
33. Flesh Grinder
34. Gore Beyond Necropsy
35. Brutal Nasty Gore
36. Butcher ABC
37. Carnivore Diprosopus
38. Severe Torture
39. Gorerotted
40. Splatterhouse
41. Lord Gore
42. Gutted
43. Terrorizer
44. Terrorist
45. The Berzerker
46. World Downfall
47. Infantiphagia
48. Eviscerated Remnants
49. Carbonized 16 Year Old Victim
50. Gory Gory Halleluja
51. Last Days of Humanity

28 BANDS WITH BLOODY NAMES

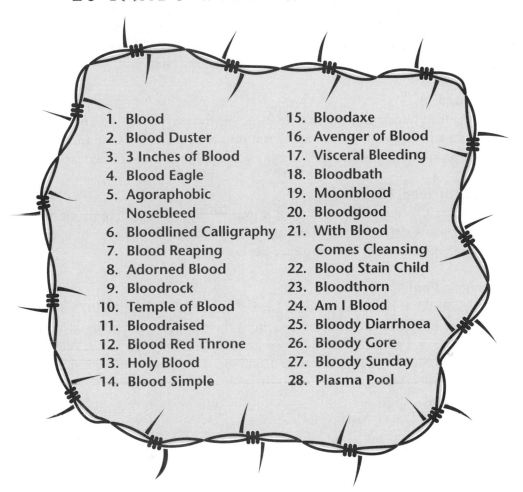

1. Blood
2. Blood Duster
3. 3 Inches of Blood
4. Blood Eagle
5. Agoraphobic Nosebleed
6. Bloodlined Calligraphy
7. Blood Reaping
8. Adorned Blood
9. Bloodrock
10. Temple of Blood
11. Bloodraised
12. Blood Red Throne
13. Holy Blood
14. Blood Simple
15. Bloodaxe
16. Avenger of Blood
17. Visceral Bleeding
18. Bloodbath
19. Moonblood
20. Bloodgood
21. With Blood Comes Cleansing
22. Blood Stain Child
23. Bloodthorn
24. Am I Blood
25. Bloody Diarrhoea
26. Bloody Gore
27. Bloody Sunday
28. Plasma Pool

12 People Who Found Themselves on the Business End of Sharon Osbourne

Sharon Osbourne's father, Don Arden, one of the most notorious managers in show business, led Black Sabbath's career in the late '70s. Sharon began dating Ozzy Osbourne shortly after he was fired from Sabbath in 1979, and Ozzy fired Arden so Sharon could manage him. Don was, needless to say, pissed off. When a pregnant Sharon arrived at her father's house one day, he sicced his dogs on her, causing her to suffer a miscarriage. She finally broke off contact with Arden after he left Sharon's mother for a younger American woman named Meredith. Although the pair didn't speak for twenty years, she was, apparently, still Daddy's Girl. . . .

1. Don Arden

Ozzy Osbourne said in an interview that during the period Sharon and her father were estranged, she would occasionally run into him in public. One time, he says, when Sharon spotted him, she tried to run over him in public, with her car.

2. Don's Girlfriend, Meredith

Another time, Ozzy recalls, when Sharon was at the Polo Lounge in the Beverly Hills Hotel, she spotted Meredith having dinner. Sharon walked over to Meredith's table and poured a bowl of hot soup over her head.

3. Lynsey de Paul

Don Arden took on British pop singer Lynsey de Paul as a client in 1973. Financial discrepancies in Arden's accounting destroyed their professional relationship a few years later, and de Paul told Arden his services were no longer required. When word of this reached Sharon, she went into de Paul's room and pissed in her suitcase.

4. Elton John

Sharon's brother David Arden told the *News of the World* newspaper that back in the early '70s, Sharon and Elton John once tried to bed the same man. When Elton came out on top, so to speak, Sharon was so furious she drove to his mansion, took a dump in his driveway, and smeared her shit all over his Rolls-Royce.

5. David Arden

David also recalled sending Ozzy a friendly note after the time Ozzy was arrested for strangling Sharon. A few days later, Arden received a hand-delivered Tiffany box. When he opened it up, he found the note he'd sent to Ozzy, which Sharon had used to wipe her ass.

6. Don Arden, again

After finding a stuffed toy Arden had been given by a mistress, Sharon showed her displeasure by smearing shit on the doll's head and putting it outside their front door so her father would find it.

7. John Scher

For a profile on her father appearing in the *Independent* newspaper, Robert Chalmers asked Sharon what she learned from her father's mistakes. "You cannot go around issuing threats," she said. "There are other ways of dealing with people." When Chalmers next mentioned John Scher, Sharon responded, "Who? That idiot that staged the last Woodstock? He was trying to take advantage. So I kicked him in the balls, and I head-butted him."

8. Korn manager

Sharon also admitted in that interview to an encounter with Korn's day-to-day manager during Ozzfest in 2002. "He touched me. Not in a sexual way, but in a condescending way," she explained. Her reaction? "I kicked him, and he fell down the stairs."

9. Bruce Dickinson

Sharon's most public display of aggression came during Iron Maiden's last gig at Ozzfest in 2005. She claimed that Bruce Dickinson had been bad-mouthing Ozzy from the stage every night, despite the fact they were being paid $185,000 a gig. "The band are real nice guys," she said, "but the singer has a chip on his shoulder. He never once thanked us for the tour. People don't act like that." To show Dickinson how people *do* act, Sharon recruited two hundred accomplices, including her daughter Kelly and some people who worked at the hospital where Sharon had recently been treated for colon cancer, to pelt him with eggs. "This one guy got [Dickinson] with a fucking egg right in the middle of his brow," she laughed later. "What a star!"

10–11. Bob Daisley and Lee Kerslake

The original bassist and drummer on Ozzy's *Diary of a Madman* had their parts rerecorded by Robert Trujillo and Mike Bordin, respectively, for the album's 2002 CD reissue. At a press conference promoting the release, Sharon said that "because of Daisley and Kerslake's abusive and unjust behavior, Ozzy wanted to remove them from these recordings. We turned a negative into a positive by adding a fresh sound to the original albums."

12. Megan Hauserman

Sharon scrapped with the *Playboy* model/reality show regular during the finale episode of the reality dating show *Rock of Love: Charm School*. Hauserman, a castoff from the previous season of *Rock of Love with Bret Michaels*, had just dissed another contestant who'd had an operation so she couldn't bear children. Osbourne told Hauserman she should do the same, "because I don't think you should allowed to breed, my dear. One of you is enough for any country." Hauserman then made the mistake of insulting Ozzy, at which point Sharon picked up a glass, threw its contents in square Hauserman's face, and—according to the police report filed later—scratched Hauserman and clawed her weave till they were separated by security. Sharon and Hauserman, not Hauserman and her weave . . .

Metal Poet Yoko Kinzoku's History of Van Halen Feuds in Haiku

1. Van Halen vs. David Lee Roth

Lion-maned rock god
What's with the Diamond Dave act?
Not in this band, man

2. Van Halen vs. Sammy Hagar

Bringer of pop rock
Our guitar shred will return
With or without you

3. Van Halen vs. David Lee Roth, redux

TV reunion
Hyping greatest hits CD
Doesn't mean you're back

4. Van Halen vs. Gary Cherone

Thinking man's singer
Good idea, no hard feelings
What's Dave's number, Ed?

5. Van Halen vs. Michael Anthony

Reunion with Dave!
Wolfgang's going to play bass!
Like Hagar now, dude?

Japanese-American metal poet Yoko Kinzoku is the world's foremost proponent of metal haiku (haiku metaru). She has penned more than six hundred stanzas about the musical form and is compiling her first collection.

7 Metalheads Who Were Injured Onstage

1. Gene Simmons (Kiss)

Paul Stanley once said of the band's New Year's Eve 1973 gig at Manhattan's Academy of Music, "There was absolutely no doubt in any of our minds that we weren't going to blow everybody off the stage." Little did he know how right he'd be. . . . For one brief, shining moment, Gene Simmons was the hottest member of the Hottest Band in the Land when his hair caught fire during his signature move, breathing fire at the end of "Firehouse." A roadie ran onstage and quickly snuffed out the blaze, and Gene wasn't seriously hurt. It wasn't the last time Simmons would light up the stage, either. It happened again during the 1976 Destroyer tour, and once again in Japan in 1977.

2. Ace Frehley (Kiss)

When *Guitar World* magazine asked Frehley to recall his most embarrassing onstage moment, he said, "Getting electrocuted in Lakeland, Florida, during the *Destroyer* tour. It was right before Kiss got wireless guitars. I was walking down these steps onstage with those very high-heeled boots. I grabbed the railing because I was losing my balance. The railing wasn't grounded properly and I got zapped with 240 volts. I saw sparks and don't remember much else. I was told the roadies carried me offstage. I had burns on my hand and the band had to stop the show. When I finally regained consciousness, I couldn't feel my right hand. It was scary." Not one to ignore a flash of inspiration, Frehley used the incident as the basis for his song "Shock Me."

3. Jimmy Page (Led Zeppelin)

Led Zeppelin's final, 1977 U.S. tour experienced several incidents of firecrackers being thrown by the crowd. Before the band played their first note at the Chicago Pavilion on April 6, Robert Plant had to ask the audience to stop throwing firecrackers; later in the evening he yelled, "Hey, cool the explosives!" No one was hurt that night, but on June 14, the last show of a six-night stand at Madison Square Garden, Page was hit on the hand with a firecracker. (Ironically, a newspaper article by David Farrell published earlier that day mentioned how the previous five NYC gigs had been violence free.) Plant scolded the crowd soon afterwards, saying, "What a terrible way to end six beautiful nights." That was true in more ways than one; the show was the last performance the original line-up gave in the Big Apple. Almost three years later to the day, Page caught a firecracker in the face in Vienna, Austria, while playing "White Summer." A few minutes after Page walked offstage, an announcer came out and said that he wanted the person who threw the fireworks "up heah [at

the stage] before de show goes on. I cannot leef him in d'audience. . . . Ve vant to talk to heem. So zee neighbors should get him here. Yes! Because dis ee-diot just shtopped the show for all de others!"

4. Tommy Lee (Mötley Crüe)

While playing Wyoming in 2005, Lee was burned on the arm and face by a pyro-technic explosion gone bad while flying between two drum kits suspended above the audience. Lee, surprisingly enough, went back and played one more song before seeking medical help. Vince Neil later said, "He didn't look too good while the paramedics were treating him backstage, so we chose to err on the side of caution and send him to the hospital."

5. Slipknot

The various members of Slipknot have earned, between them, lacerated shins, shin splints, slipped vertebrae, dislocated shoulders, broken ankles, broken toes, broken ribs, broken collarbones, headbanging-related whiplash, and concussions.

6. Burton C. Bell (Fear Factory)

Fear Factory's front man had a hair-raising experience during the band's first-ever show in Luxembourg: onstage electrocution during the song "Archetype." A series of electrical mishaps had been causing the power and sound to cut out during the night, and as the end of the show approached, he touched the mic and was knocked off his feet. Bell was carried offstage and tended to by some roadies, none of whom bothered to call for medical help.

7. Alice Cooper

When he was drinking, it wasn't unusual for Alice to perform with broken bones from either falling down or even tumbling off the stage. His famous hanging finale took a nasty turn one night when the cables attached to the vest that kept him suspended snapped, causing him to hit the trapdoor with his chin, knocking him unconscious. The injuries continued even after his drinking stopped. He broke 12 ribs after tripping on a wire in Vancouver and falling 12 feet into the audience. One night he tried to put his favorite sword, which once belonged to Errol Flynn, back into its scabbard but missed the scabbard and rammed the blade through his leg. In August 2008, the sixty-year-old Cooper was performing in Oregon when he fell off the stage, cracking a rib and incurring cartilage damage. He kept playing and didn't go to the doctor for days.

126 Metal Band Names That Have to Do with . . . Death or Dying!

1. Autopsy
2. Death Stars
3. As I Lay Dying
4. Automatized Cyborg Death
5. Necro Ginecologo Canibal
6. Canibalismo Gourmet
7. Daylight Dies
8. Necroabortion
9. Cannibal Corpse
10. Cemetary
11. Ancient Necropsy
12. Death
13. Armageddon
14. Cianide
15. Circle of Dead Children
16. Dead Horse
17. Coffins
18. Murder Squad
19. Autopsy Torment
20. Deathbound
21. My Dying Bride
22. Demisor
23. Napalm Death
24. Necrodeath
25. Carcass
26. Dead Infection
27. Angel Corpse
28. Necrophagia
29. Annihilator
30. Dry Kill Logic
31. Ante Mortem
32. Deathstar
33. Deceased
34. Cadaver
35. DeadStar Assembly
36. Necro Tampon
37. Entombed
38. Deicide
39. Animals Killing People
40. Dropdead
41. Necropodridal Cadaveric
42. Dublin Death Patrol
43. Hobbs' Angel of Death
44. Dying Fetus
45. Burial
46. Eternal Grave
47. Evildead
48. Lawnmower Deth
49. Gravedigger
50. Dethklok
51. Executer
52. Deathspell Omega
53. Morgue
54. Fuck … I'm Dead
55. Graveland
56. Necrocannibal
57. Mortuary Hacking Session
58. Dark Funeral
59. Coroner
60. Crematory
61. Necromance
62. Crimson Death
63. Deathchain
64. Cryptophilia
65. Death Angel
66. Mortuary Stench
67. Graveworm
68. Grim Reaper
69. Hearse
70. Funeral Mist
71. Sublime Cadaveric Decomposition
72. Hibernus Mortis (Latin for "Dead Winter")

73. Cryptosporidium Parvum
74. Holocaust
75. Necrocannibalistic Vomitorium
76. Infestdead
77. Beheaded
78. Nokturnal Mortum
79. Burial Chamber Trio
80. Mortician
81. Imago Mortis
82. Planta Cadaver
83. Post Mortem
84. Black Murder
85. Merciless Death
86. Lapidate (means "To Kill by Stoning")
87. Necrophagist
88. Grave
89. Necrophobic
90. Nuclear Death
91. Wormeaten
92. Obituary
93. Parasiticide
94. Living Death
95. The Red Death
96. Throb of Offal
97. Stormtroopers of Death
98. Between the Buried and Me
99. Necromantia
100. Offalmincer
101. Toxic Death
102. Unholy Grave
103. Six Feet Under
104. Overkill
105. Slaughterhouse
106. Slayer
107. Killwhitneydead
108. Through the Eyes of the Dead
109. Lust of Decay
110. Massacre
111. Torture Killer
112. Séance
113. Waking the Cadaver
114. Cadaver Inc.
115. Terminally Your Aborted Ghost
116. Snuffgrinder
117. Zombie Ritual
118. Suffocation
119. To/Die/For
120. Memento Mori
121. Ripping Corpse
122. Short Bus Pile Up
123. The County Medical Examiners
124. Megadeth
125. Suicidal Tendencies
126. The Funeral Pyre

9 Metal Suicides

1. Wendy O. Williams (Plasmatics)

Williams was a vegetarian animal-rights activist who helped run a Connecticut health food store after Plasmatics ended. The singer committed suicide with a shotgun in 1998, at the age of forty-eight.

2. Sergey Kudishin (Cherniy Kofe, translates to "Black Coffee")

Jumped off a balcony in 1993.

3. Max "Mad Max" Varnier (Kult, Beer Vomit, and Worship)

Mad Max killed himself by jumping off a bridge in 2001.

4. Dan "Cernunnos" Vandenplas (Enthroned)

Cernunnos hung himself two weeks shy of his twenty-sixth birthday.

5. Steve MacDonald (Gorguts)

The drummer hanged himself.

6. Clifford Davies

A drummer and producer for Ted Nugent from 1975 to 1982, Davies was found dead on April 15, 2008 in Atlanta of a self-inflicted gunshot wound. The night before his suicide he called the owner of the recording studio where he worked, upset about mounting medical bills.

7. Jon Nodtveidt (Dissection)

The guitarist shot himself in 2006.

8. Stephen S. Sherwood (Immortal Dominion)

Shot himself after he shot and killed his wife.

9. Ingo Schwichtenberg (Helloween)

After drug addiction and schizophrenia contributed to his being kicked out of the band, he jumped in front of a subway train.

3 Metal Bands Cleared of Causing Someone's Suicide or Murder

1. Judas Priest

The parents of two depressed Judas Priest fans involved in a suicide pact blamed subliminal messages embedded on the track "Better By You, Better Than Me" for telling their kids to "do it, do it." (One teen succeeded in doing it, while the other was permanently disfigured and disabled.) During the trial, the band's manager claimed, "I'd be saying 'Buy seven copies [of our record],' not telling a couple of screwed-up kids to kill themselves." A judge found that whatever backwards message did exist was coincidental and had nothing to do with the doomed teens' suicide pact.

2. Ozzy Osbourne

Osbourne has been implicated in two suicides, and cleared of responsibility in both. In one case, a nineteen-year-old man shot himself in the head while listening to Ozzy's song "Suicide Solution," which is actually about the death of AC/DC's Bon Scott. Two years later the young man's parents sued, claiming that Ozzy's video "Don't Blame Me" contained tones that made their son susceptible to the subliminal commands to shoot himself contained in "Suicide Solution."

3. Slayer

Fifteen-year-old Elyse Pahler was stabbed to death by three members of California metal band Hatred, drug abusers and Slayer fans who reportedly sacrificed her to Satan to help them gain success. The men confessed to the crime and were sentenced to prison. Pahler's parents later sued the band, saying their lyrics drove the killers to action, seeking money and a ban on marketing the band's albums to minors. A judge threw the case out, saying that while Slayer's music is "destructive," it was not the cause of Pahler's death. The killers were.

25 BANDS NAMED AFTER . . . MENTAL DEFECT OR DISEASE!

1. Mental Horror
2. Excruciating Terror
3. Abysmal Torment
4. Deranged
5. Anorexia Nervosa
6. Autophagia
7. Clutch Mental Hospital
8. Coprophagia Nervosa
9. Alienation Mental
10. Dead Brain Cells
11. Katatonia
12. Decrepit Birth
13. Detrimentum
14. Enmity
15. Phobia
16. Repulsion
17. Ignorance
18. Hydrophobia
19. Misery
20. Pathology
21. Lividity
22. Internal Suffering
23. Infernal Torment
24. Freakhate
25. Lack of Interest

6 Metalheads Who Have Worn Straitjackets

1. Alice Cooper
Alice made the straitjacket must-wear rock 'n' roll gear with the song "The Ballad of Dwight Frye."

2. Ozzy Osbourne
Ozzy has strapped one on in promotional photos, and markets a caricature wearing one as well.

3. Jon Oliva's Pain
The band, minus Oliva, wear straitjackets on the cover of the CD *Straight-Jacket Memoir*.

4. Kevin DuBrow (Quiet Riot)
That's Kevin wearing one in the video for "Bang Your Head" and on the cover of the album *Metal Health*.

5. Kiss
The group appear in straitjackets in a poster and on a Christmas-themed T-shirt.

6. Eddie
The Iron Maiden mascot appears all wrapped up as an action figure.

12 Metal Songs About Serial Killers
1. "Ted Bundy"—Coven
2. "Taste the Pain"—Church of Misery (about Graham Young)
3. "Mr. Albert Fish (Was Children Your Favorite Dish?)"—Macabre
4. "The Night Stalker"—Bewitched (about Richard Ramirez)
5. "Jumping at Shadows"—Benediction (the lyrics come from Son of Sam letters)
6. "Mr. Arnold Palmer? Nice Meal for Jeffrey Dahmer"—Godstomper
7. "Manson Klan"—Righteous Pigs
8. "Sniper in the Sky—Macabre (about Charles Whitman)

9. "Henry: Portrait of a Serial Killer"—Fantômas (about Henry Lee Lucas)
10. "33 Something"—Bathory (about John Wayne Gacy)
11. "The Ripper"—Judas Priest (about Jack The Ripper)
12. "To Catch a Killer (a Serial Sing-a-Long)"—Gorerotted (sung from the point of view of John Wayne Gacy, Jack the Ripper, Ted Bundy, Fred West, and John George Haigh)

8 Metalheads Who Were Murdered

1. Hamilton Castro (Neurosis Inc.)
Shot when someone tried to steal his bike.

2. "Dimebag" Darrell Abbott (Pantera, Damageplan)
Dimebag was shot to death on December 8, 2004, seconds after taking the stage with Damageplan by a deranged fan who blamed him for Pantera's breakup.

3. Kevin O'Brien (Spandex Caravan)
Killed during a robbery in 2008.

4. Rhett Forrester (Riot)
Shot to death in Atlanta in 1994. His murder remains unsolved.

5. Dave Holocaust (Destructor)
Stabbed by a drunk at a New Year's Eve party in 1988.

6. Henrik Johansson (Apostasy)
Stabbed by his girlfriend in 2006.

7. Eric Roy (Apathy)
He was murdered in 2001.

8. Gregory Greenawalt (Relic)
Shot after an argument.

Under My Wheels: 13 Metalheads Who Died in Vehicle Accidents

1. Razzle (Hanoi Rocks)
The glam rock drummer was killed in a drunk driving accident on December 8, 1984. Mötley Crüe's Vince Neil was the drunk driving.

2. Rob Sterzel (Deceased)
Killed in a hit-and-run accident.

3. Christopher Zimmermann (Rammstein touring bassist)
The DC-9 plane he was in exploded after takeoff.

4. Flipper Schwartz (Scobeys)
His truck hit a semitrailer in 2006.

5. Audie Pitre (Acid Bath)
Killed by a drunk driver.

6. Tim Kelly (Slaughter)
Succumbed to head injuries from a crash with an eighteen-wheeler.

7. Theo Loomans (Asphyx)
His car was hit by a train.

8. Brittany Allsopp (Idol Worship)
Died at the age of seventeen in a car accident.

9. Ron Johnson (Salem's Wych)
He was killed in a motorcycle accident.

10. Jacek Regulski (Kat)
The guitarist died in a motorcycle accident in 1999.

11. Cliff Burton (Metallica)

The bassist died in a tour bus accident in 1986.

12. David Rairan (Purulent)

The guitarist died in 2003 of injuries sustained in a tour bus crash.

13. Damo Morris (Red Shore)

The singer died in 2007 after his van hit a tree.

Metal's 5 Gnarliest Deaths

1. Gunther Deitz

The singer dove off the stage during a concert, the crowd moved away and he landed headfirst on the concrete floor.

2. Shawn Kettlewell (Prolific)

The drummer died in 2006 when he was hit by a car battery that had been ejected from a single-car accident on the other side of the freeway.

3. Randy Rhoads (Quiet Riot, Blizzard of Ozz)

The guitarist was killed while horsing around in a plane in 1982. The pilot was showing off with some fancy flying when the wing of the plane struck Ozzy's tour bus. Both Ozzy and Sharon witnessed the crash.

4. Kurt Struebing (NME)

Struebing's car fell through the opening of a drawbridge in 2005.

5. Bohdan Furch (Argema)

Furch was electrocuted onstage.

The 5 Dead Spinal Tap Drummers

These men truly made rock history when they dared sit behind the drum kit of Spinal Tap.

1. John "Stumpy" Pepys
Stumpy is now pushing up the daisies after his death in a gardening accident.

2. Eric "Stumpy Joe" Childs
Choked on "somebody else's vomit."

3. Peter "James" Bond
Yet another tragic rock 'n' roll case of spontaneous combustion.

4. Mick Shrimpton
Exploded onstage (his death was captured in the film *This Is Spinal Tap*).

5. Joe "Mama" Besser
Missing and presumed dead.

Dave Brockie (a.k.a. Oderus Urungus of Gwar)'s 10 Sickest Things to Ever Happen at a Gwar Show

1. Dead Animals Get Thrown at the Band
At various shows in Gwar's career, the band has been pelted with a dead cat with an eyeball hanging out of its socket, a pair of dead sharks, a dead baby chicken, and a dead armadillo.

2. A Vomit Barrage
While Gwar were performing at the infamous "Vera" squat in Groningen, Holland, the locals showed their love for the band by pelting us with cups of rotten dog vomit.

3. On with the Show
After suffering a near-fatal gunshot wound in an attempted carjacking in Washington, D.C., guitarist Flattus Maximus (Pete Lee) continued to tour, even though he had a full colostomy bag, which he often filled while the band played.

4. The Ultimate Sacrifice
During a show at Oakland's Omni Theater, a member of the crowd suffered a fatal neck injury after he got crushed by a boots-first balcony diver. Years later at a beach party in the area, a girl who had been hanging out with the band proudly revealed that she was the one responsible for the man's death.

5. Another Argument for Shaved Heads

During a particularly violent show, an unfortunate audience member was thrown up on the stage, inextricably winding his long hair around bassist Casey Orr (a.k.a. Beefcake the Mighty)'s tuning keys. As he stood there, helpless, he proceeded to absorb blow after heavy blow to the face as angry band members vented their frustration upon him. This continued until a Gwar slave appeared with a huge pair of scissors and de-maned the poor kid with a single stroke.

6. Up to the Elbow

The show at L.A.'s Palace Theatre was going smoothly enough until I turned around and noticed one of the opening bands' tour managers, in full view of the audience, attempting to ram his entire arm into the vagina of some passed-out chick on the side of the stage.

7. The Pause That Refreshes

After a hot show in Italy, Gwar's representative of the fairer sex, Danielle Stampe (a.k.a. Slymenstra Hymen), hurried backstage to cool off. Upending a bottle of weird European water over her head, she quickly realized that someone had filled the bottle with hot man-pee.

8. Wooden You Know It?

At a show at the infamously inadequate Jax in Springfield, Virginia, band members were horrified to see a barricade had been shoddily constructed out of flimsy wooden 2 × 2's. It was almost instantly destroyed by the moshing crowd, leaving broken stakes jutting into the crowd at eye level. Impalement was barely avoided by Gwar slaves wrapping foam rubber and duct tape around the jagged ends.

9. A Shocking Experience

While performing at the unbelievably crappy Insect Club in Norfolk, Virginia, while drunk as hell, I reached up and grabbed an ungrounded lighting truss, blowing myself several feet through the air until I crashed into the drum set.

10. The Show Itself

Undoubtedly the sickest thing to ever happen at a Gwar show is . . . a Gwar show!

A founding member of Gwar, Dave Brockie switched from playing guitar to becoming a vocalist, for better or worse.

Pirate Radio Pioneer Dave Rabbit's *Radio First Termer* Playlist

For three weeks in 1971, U.S.A.F. Sgt. "Dave Rabbit" and two sidekicks broadcast a pirate radio show, *Radio First Termer*, from the back of a Saigon whorehouse to "bring back rock 'n' roll to the troops on the front lines." The show regularly featured comedy skits insulting commanding officers; gave young, greenhorn soldiers (the "first termers") tips on where to score good dope and disease-free hookers; and generally fought the establishment with heavy acid rock/metal as its ammo. One three-hour episode was recorded and made its way back to the States, where copies were sold in underground magazines and head shops.

1. "Fancy Space Odyssey"—Bloodrock

This was a little-known and rarely heard cut that I just happened to love. I was a huge Bloodrock fan and couldn't play enough of their stuff.

2. "Gotta Find a Way"—Bloodrock

I used "Gotta Find a Way" because I always tied the song to my slogan, "Gotta Find a Way to Get Out of Fuckin' Vietnam."

3. "Dead on Arrival"—Bloodrock

Although "Dead on Arrival" was a gory song to be playing for the troops, they really loved it. It's the perfect "let's laugh at death" song because it emulated exactly what the troops were going through on a day-to-day basis in the rice paddies and jungles of Vietnam.

4. "Double Cross"—Bloodrock

I normally always started each show with "Double Cross" because of the significance of the title; 1971 was a time of huge anti-war sentiment within the ranks of the soldiers there, and with over 500,000 desertions—by the Pentagon's own admission—there were few "first termers" who didn't think they were being "double-crossed."

5. "Born to Be Wild"—Steppenwolf

I always considered myself "Born to Be Wild," as did every troop, who had an average age of nineteen. There wasn't a more fitting song for *Radio First Termer* to play to pump up the morale of the troops that were dreading another day in 'Nam.

6. "Don't Step on the Grass, Sam"—Steppenwolf

Marijuana use in the field was rampant. Fighting bloody battles day and night, most military commanders turned their heads as their battle-worn troops put a little Mary Jane in their life. Although cohosts Pete Sadler, Nguyen, and I always did our shows straight, I'd light up a cigarette with my Zippo and click the lid loudly, giving the troops the impression that I was toking it up right there with them. It was this mental image that brought the troops and me extremely close over those twenty-one nights.

7. "The Pusher"—Steppenwolf

I use to get tips from my network of friends about all kinds of drug-related stuff and would use "The Pusher" as a springboard to pass those tips along, live on the air.

8. "Fire"—Jimi Hendrix

I don't think a show went by that we didn't include at least a couple of Jimi Hendrix songs. "Fire" was in my top two. The artillery troops loved it especially because it contained their prime command word: "Fire!" Almost every night I'd dedicate the song to the artillery troops throughout Vietnam.

9. "Purple Haze"—Jimi Hendrix

"Purple Haze" is my all-time favorite Hendrix song. I tried to play it nightly if possible because it portrayed lyrically what I was experiencing personally with my own demons during three tours of Vietnam.

10. "Changes"—Jimi Hendrix and the Band of Gypsies

Radio First Termer introduced Buddy Miles to the troops in Vietnam. I found out about Buddy during his Jimi Hendrix days. "Changes" was a great song, as it totally described what a lot of the "cherry troops" (fresh meat new to 'Nam) were feeling. The cherries were the first to go into battle and the last ones to leave. There were over 58,000 deaths in Vietnam; the majority of them were first termers and cherries.

11. "Good Times, Bad Times"—Led Zeppelin

From the very first cut to the last of Led Zeppelin's debut album, I was hooked and hooked bad. Not only did their hard, acid rock music fit perfectly with what I was trying to do with *Radio First Termer*, the lyrics were right on target, with me as well as with the thousands of troops throughout Vietnam, Cambodia, and Laos.

12. "Heartbreaker"—Led Zeppelin

"Heartbreaker" was my teaser song. I played it every show and would dedicate it to the new troops who had just recently come in country. When I was stationed at Cam Ranh Bay, which was the main entry and exit point for military personnel in Vietnam, I could relive that feeling of watching the civilian aircraft lift off with troops flying back home after surviving a tour. It was, indeed, a "Heartbreaker."

13. "My Flash on You"—Love

Love wasn't a widely popular band during this period of time, but I identified with this one song greatly. It's the only Love song that was played on *Radio First Termer*.

14. "Soul Experience"—Iron Butterfly

As far as I'm concerned, Iron Butterfly never got their due despite their unique, groundbreaking style. The first time I heard "Soul Experience," I was mesmerized by the music and the lyrics about being yourself. If ever there was a theme song for Dave Rabbit and *Radio First Termer*, this was it.

15. "In-A-Gadda-Da-Vida"—Iron Butterfly

It's pissing down rain. The only thing keeping you dry is a makeshift tarp over your head. You have your portable radio, covered in cellophane, and you're tuned in to Dave Rabbit's nightly broadcast of *Radio First Termer*. All of a sudden, you hear Iron Butterfly's "In-A-Gadda-Da-Vida" (the long version, of course). Suddenly, everything seems right with world. You have a renewed hope that you just might make it home. That's why I loved this song so much; it spoke to the hearts and minds of the soldiers in combat.

16. "You Keep Me Hanging On"—Vanilla Fudge

Radio First Termer used to play a lot of Vanilla Fudge. But of all of the songs from their catalog that I had access to, none was more popular or requested than "You Keep Me Hanging On." It reminded all the troops of the loves, family, and friends who were their sole motivations for surviving 'Nam and maybe, just maybe, of being reunited with them when they returned home.

Dave Rabbit learned of existence of the Radio First Termer *tape while helping his son research a school paper online. Since going public, he's been hailed as the father of pirate radio, has been interviewed by Opie & Anthony, and appears in the antiwar documentary* Sir! No Sir! *In 2006, Rabbit and two new cohosts revived the show and did a thirty-fifth anniversary show for the troops in Iraq. He now broadcasts* The ATS Mix Show.

4 Metal Bands with an Unusual, Coincidental Connection to 9/11 (and One Honorable Mention)

1. Slayer
The band's album *God Hates Us All* was released on September 11, 2001, and included the songs "Disciple," "God Send Death," "War Zone," "Here Comes the Pain," and "Payback."

2. Otep
The band's EP *Jihad* was released less than three months before the attack and included the song "The Lord Is My Weapon." The band had to change the name of the EP in some markets, removing the word *jihad* from the cover.

3. System of a Down
Down's second CD, *Toxicity*, was released a week before the attacks and was sitting at number one on the *Billboard* charts on September 11, 2001. It included the song "Chop Suey!" which had the line, "Trust in my self-righteous suicide."

4. Shihad
The New Zealand metal band made the decision to rechristen themselves after 9/11, first going with Remote and then Pacifier, so their name wouldn't be mistaken with the word *jihad*. In 2004 they went back to Shihad, which they had originally gotten from the David Lynch movie *Dune*.

Honorable Mention

Anthrax
When five people were killed after the 9/11 attacks by letters containing anthrax, conventional wisdom had the speed metallers changing their name. On October 10, 2001, the band issued a press release joking they might choose "something more friendly," like "Basket Full of Puppies." The release continued, "To us and to millions of people, [Anthrax] is just a name. We don't want to change the name of the band, not because it would be a pain in the ass, but because we hope that no further negative events will happen and it won't be necessary. We hope and pray that this problem goes away quietly and we all grow old and fat together." A month later Anthrax played a benefit show for families of police and firemen killed on September 11. Each member wore a white jumpsuit with a different word printed on it. When they stood in the right order, the outfits said, "We're Not Changing Our Name."

48 Metal Songs That Clear Channel Communications "Suggested" Their Radio Stations Avoid Playing After the September 11, 2001, Terror Attacks (And One Honorable Mention)

1. "Safe in New York City"—AC/DC
2. "Enter Sandman"—Metallica
3. "Bad Day"—Fuel
4. "Bad Religion"—Godsmack
5. "Sabbath Bloody Sabbath"—Black Sabbath
6. "War Pigs"—Black Sabbath
7. "Killer Queen"—Queen
8. "Rooster"—Alice in Chains
9. "Blow Up the Outside World"—Soundgarden
10. "Chop Suey!"—System of a Down
11. "Holy Diver"—Dio
12. "Suicide Solution"—Ozzy Osbourne
13. "Seek & Destroy"—Metallica
14. "Boom"—P.O.D.
15. "TNT"—AC/DC
16. "Click Click Boom"—Saliva
17. "Death Blooms"—Mudvayne
18. "Wait and Bleed"—Slipknot
19. "Burnin' for You"—Blue Öyster Cult
20. "Fire Woman"—the Cult
21. "Bodies"—Drowning Pool
22. "Jump"—Van Halen
23. "Falling Away from Me"—Korn
24. "Fell on Black Days"—Soundgarden
25. "Down in a Hole"—Alice in Chains
26. "Another One Bites the Dust"—Queen
27. "Shot Down in Flames"—AC/DC
28. "Left Behind"—Slipknot
29. "Knockin' on Heaven's Door"—Guns N' Roses
30. "Stairway to Heaven"—Led Zeppelin
31. "Highway to Hell"—AC/DC
32. "Black Hole Sun"—Soundgarden
33. "Sea of Sorrow"—Alice in Chains

34. "Dancing in the Street"—Van Halen
35. "Intolerence"—Tool
36. "Hey Joe"—the Jimi Hendrix Experience
37. "Break Stuff"—Limp Bizkit
38. "Dirty Deeds Done Dirt Cheap"—AC/DC
39. "Harvester of Sorrow"—Metallica
40. "Smooth Criminal"—Alien Ant Farm
41. "Sweating Bullets"—Megadeth
42. "Some Heads Are Gonna Roll"—Judas Priest
43. "Shoot to Thrill"—AC/DC
44. "Dread and the Fugitive Mind"—Megadeth
45. "Head Like a Hole"—Nine Inch Nails
46. "Them Bones"—Alice in Chains
47. "Hells Bells"—AC/DC
48. "Fade to Black"—Metallica

Honorable Mention
All songs by Rage Against the Machine

8 Heavy Metal Songs the Government Has Used to Torture Prisoners at Abu Ghraib and Guantánamo Bay

In the March/April 2008 issue of *Mother Jones* magazine, investigative journalist Justine Sharrock published the article "Am I a Torturer?" The author spoke with former soldiers and guards at several Iraqi prisons, including Abu Ghraib, as well as Cuba's Guantánamo Bay about the repetitive use of excessively loud music ("no-touch torture") on prisoners. According to her interview subjects—both soldiers and prisoners—as well as "a leaked interrogation log," here are some the metal songs they used.

1. "Bulls on Parade"—Rage Against the Machine
2. "Fuck Your God"—Deicide
3. "Bodies"—Drowning Pool
4. "Take Your Best Shot"—Dope
5. "Shoot to Thrill"—AC/DC
6. "Die Motherfucker Die"—Dope
7. "Click Click Boom"—Saliva
8. "Enter Sandman"—Metallica

William Murderface of Dethklok's Top 5 Most Metal Civil War Generals

5. Zebulon York (1819–1900)

Zebulon! What a cool fucking name! It's like he was from outer space.... And he graduated from fucking Transylvania University of Kentucky! What the fuck?! Now that's metal!

4. Daniel Ruggles (1810–1897)

Ruggles had the *hugest* fucking beard of the Civil War, and everyone knows that long hair is metal.

3. Stonewall Jackson (1824–1863)

This guy was insane! Just look into his eyes. Definitely metal.

2. Maxcy Gregg (1814–1862)

Tell me that name doesn't sound like a great fuckin' Southern metal band. Ladies and gentlemen, Maxcy Gregg! And he was fucking shot in the spine! Metal.

1. Ulysses S. Grant (1822–1885)

In 1864, he made a brutal fucking mistake at Cold Harbor and got 7,000 dudes killed in half an hour. Plus he was a drunk! METAL!

Dethklok bassist William Murderface is a Civil War buff and memorabilia collector, and he's fuckin' metal.

CHAPTER 4

✖
(SEX/⊕BSCENI✝Y)

10 Heavy Metal Celebrity Sex Tapes

1. Pam Anderson and Tommy Lee

The most notorious celebrity sex tape of them all. Often mislabeled a "honeymoon" tape, it was actually filmed during Pam's birthday celebration and, along with some dirty Polaroids and love letters, was stashed in a safe that was later stolen from the pair's house by a disgruntled electrician. The inevitable bootleg copies became an instant hit. Celebrities held invite-only viewing parties in the Hollywood Hills, and anyone not connected enough to score their own free copy paid $100 for it on the black market. It all seemed just a bit of fun until Internet Entertainment Group, a California porn company, announced they were going to market it online. The pair sued the company but lost the case by turning the tape into a "news item" with their own interviews about it. A deal was struck whereby IEG would release the tape, with Pam and Tommy getting an undisclosed sum of money and having footage where they smoke pot edited out. *Pam & Tommy Lee: Hardcore and Uncensored* is the best-selling porn tape ever.

2. Pam Anderson and Bret Michaels

Before she was with Tommy Lee, Pam was videotaped having sex with then-boyfriend Bret Michaels of Poison after a Halloween party (Bret was dressed like

Jack the Ripper and Pam was dressed like, well, Pam). After the success of the Pam and Tommy Lee tape, the Pam and Bret tape was leaked and also offered for sale on the Internet. In an unusual but ultimately successful legal move, the pair sued for copyright infringement and won an injunction against its sale, but it was too late. The tape, like Pam's legs when there's a rock star in the room, had spread far and wide.

3. Vince Neil and Janine

After the success of *Pam & Tommy Lee: Hardcore and Uncensored*, IEG came up with this little gem, featuring Tommy Lee's bandmate Vince Neil with Penthouse Pet and porn star Janine Lindemulder. The draw of this one was twofold: another member of Mötley Crüe was caught with his pants down, and it the first time career lesbian Janine had sex with a man on film. As with the Pam and Tommy Lee tape, Lindemulder and Neil were compensated for their appearances, but the third wheel in the tape didn't sign a release and had her face obscured throughout. She was later revealed to be Penthouse Pet Brandy Ledford.

4. Evan Seinfeld and Tera Patrick

Evan and Tera are the king and queen of celebrity sex tapes, thanks to Patrick's career in the adult-film industry and Seinfeld's willingness to do whatever it takes to help her out, including becoming her onscreen partner. The pair have "worked together" about a dozen times, in titles including *Reign of Tera*, *Teradise Island 1*, *Teradise Island 2*, and *Tera Tera Tera*.

5. Gene Simmons and Traci Anna Koval

About a minute of video was released online from a tape featuring Gene Simmons and adult model Traci Anna Koval in February 2008. The footage was shot without Gene's knowledge about five years earlier but bought by him shortly thereafter; Koval denied leaking the tape and was never charged in the matter. A cease-and-desist order was fired off to the website offering online viewing privileges, not only stopping its release but also (wink, wink) confirming its existence. The fact that the clip hit the Web a few weeks before the third season premiere of his reality show *Gene Simmons Family Jewels*—which featured the results of the previous season's cliffhanger, a lie-detector test to determine if the Demon had actually bedded 4,800 women—was just a coincidence, of course.

6. The Jimi Hendrix Sex Tape

One of the most bizarre entries in the celebrity sex tape field claims to star none other than Jimi Hendrix. Hendrix was often seen making films with the latest rock star extravagance, the 8mm home movie camera, backstage at gigs or on the road. In 2008, porn company Vivid Entertainment released *Jimi Hendrix: The Sex Tape*, a late-'60s vintage sex loop running about ten minutes that was part of a larger, forty-five-minute documentary. The silent, color footage features "Jimi" with two white women performing every sex act you'd expect in a stag film. The documentary features testimonials to Hendrix's sexitude from none other than groupie queens Pamela Des Barres (who admits she never slept with Hendrix, although she did meet him at a photo shoot) and Cynthia Plaster Caster, who also didn't sample Hendrix's schlong but did cast his cock for one of her trademark rock star penis statues. The Hendrix estate was predictably up in arms about the release of the DVD, but failed to claim the $100,000 prize Vivid offered anyone who could prove it wasn't Jimi in the film.

7. Led Zeppelin
In his book *Stairway to Heaven: Led Zeppelin Uncensored*, Zep road manager Richard Cole lays to rest the rumor of Led Zeppelin and the mud shark. Kinda. The legendary event actually did take place at Seattle's Edgewater Inn, where guests could fish off their balconies into Elliott Bay. But it wasn't a mud shark that was reeled in, it was a red snapper, and it was indeed inserted into the snapper of a willing seventeen-year-old redhead named Jackie. But it wasn't a member of Zeppelin who did the deed, it was Cole himself. The incident was filmed by Mark Stein of Vanilla Fudge, who were also staying in the hotel at the same time, on that latest rock star extravagance, the 8mm home movie camera.

8. Fred Durst and friend
In 2005 Durst joined the growing fraternity of metal celebrities who had sex footage stolen and leaked onto the Internet. The footage in question, reportedly hacked from his Sidekick, featured him doing it for the nookie with a special female friend he bangs from behind for about three minutes.

9. Wendy O. Williams
Wendy O.'s short scene in the porn flick *Candy Goes to Hollywood* may not be a sex tape per se, but how many other times do you get to see a punk rocker–turned–metal priestess shoot Ping-Pong balls out of her pussy in a takeoff of *The Gong Show*?

10. Kid Rock and Scott Stapp
The Southern metal/hick-hop star and the former Creed singer successfully prevented porn company Red Light District from releasing footage of their bad selves

exchanging oral pleasantries with a quartet of adoring female fans. Stapp originally claimed that the video was leaked by someone out to ruin his new solo career and besides, it was "deceptively edited" and there wasn't any sex in it, anyway. Kid Rock, for his part, seemed like he couldn't give a shit, saying the video would give him some great publicity for his upcoming album *Live Trucker* and called Stapp "stupid" for letting it get stolen.

52 Band Names About . . . Pussy!

1. Hairy Pussy
2. Pussy Lover
3. Cunt Worship
4. Virgin's Cunt
5. Vaginator
6. Vulvulator
7. Cunt Roll
8. In Cunt
9. Hymen Holocaust
10. Stunning Cunts
11. Funcunt
12. Cunt Inferno
13. Wild Pussy
14. Pussy Universe
15. Vaginal Carnage
16. Infected Pussy
17. Fecalized Twat
18. Vaginal Haemorrhage
19. Puscunt
20. ToxicCunt
21. Gonorrhea Pussy
22. Cuntworm
23. Maggot Twat
24. Cunt Maggots
25. Cuntopsy
26. Sickcunt
27. Filthy Maggoty Cunt
28. Biopsycunt
29. Necrovaginal Acid Expulsion
30. Carnivorous Vagina
31. Cunt Face
32. Teen Pussy Fuckers
33. Wicked Pussy from the Wild West
34. Cunthunt 777
35. Clitoris Trafficker
36. Engorged Vaginal Abyss
37. Decomposed Cunt
38. Alabama Thunderpussy
39. Nashville Pussy
40. Baphomet's Cunt
41. Vulvathrone
42. Cuntscrape
43. Vulvectomy
44. Cuntshredder
45. Cunt Grinder
46. Cunthammer
47. Misogynist Pussyslasher
48. Vaginal Butchery
49. Vaginal Massaker
50. Necrocunt
51. Pocket Pussy Hash Pipe
52. Silly Twats

Love at First Sting: 9 Heavy Metal Bitch Magnets . . .

1. Gene Simmons

Among the five thousand women Simmons has bedded are some he'll even be seen with in public. Simmons was a tabloid darling in the '70s when he was dating Diana Ross and Cher, but paparazzi trying to photograph Simmons without makeup always came up empty since he usually hid behind a dinner napkin or hat. Simmons has been with his current non-wife, *Playboy* Playmate Shannon Tweed—whom he met at the Playboy Mansion—for almost a quarter century. The world-famous tongue that gets him all this action made headlines with another ex-girlfriend: Georgeann Walsh Ward, who dated Gene in the '70s and sued him in 2005 when comments he made on television about his sexual conquests ("There wasn't a girl that was off-limits, and I enjoyed every one of them") were juxtaposed with photos of her. The pair settled the case amicably in 2006.

2. Evan Seinfeld

Biohazard's bassist is married to porn star and erotic entrepreneur Tera Patrick. They got together after Patrick saw Seinfeld on the drama *Oz*. They got hitched in Vegas. They do porn together. Very metal.

3. Nikki Sixx

Playboy Playmate Donna D'Erico and Sixx divorced in 2007, after nine years of marriage.

4. John 5

John 5 was married to Penthouse Pet Aria Giovanni.

5. Marilyn Manson

Manson's list of lovers includes former wife Dita Von Teese, Evan Rachel Wood, and Rose McGowan.

6. Duff McKagan

Duff was married to *Playboy* Playmate Linda Johnson for four years in the early '90s.

7. Morgan Rose (Sevendust)

Rose is married to *Playboy* Playmate Teri Harrison.

8. Axl Rose (Guns N' Roses)

Rose dated supermodel Stephanie Seymour, who appeared in the video for "November Rain."

9. Jonathan Davis (Korn)

In 2004 he married former porn star Deven Davis.

. . . and 3 Bitchin' Heavy Metal Heartbreakers

1. Pamela Anderson

Pamela has said, "I'm with the band," as girlthing to Bret Michaels, Tommy Lee (whom she married and divorced), Kid Rock (whom she married and divorced), and Tommy Lee (whom reconciled with and split from).

2. Heather Locklear

Locklear was married to Tommy Lee for seven years and to Richie Sambora for eleven years.

3. Bobbie Brown

The "Cherry Pie" video girl dated Jani Lane (Warrant), Bret Michaels (Poison), Stevie Rachelle (Tuff), Jay Gordon (Orgy), and Tommy Lee, of course.

10 Smoking Hot Heavy Metal Video Vixens

1. Tawny Kitaen

The undisputed queen of hair metal video slinked her way through the Whitesnake videos "Here I Go Again," "Is This Love," and "Still of the Night." She was married to David Coverdale from 1988 to 1991. She also shows up in Ratt's "Back for More" video (she was dating guitarist Robbin Crosby) and was the cover model on Ratt's *Out of the Cellar*.

2. Bobbie Brown

The blonde we all wanted to fuck in Warrant's "Cherry Pie" clip also appeared in "Once Bitten, Twice Shy" by Great White.

3–4. Traci Lords and Brinke Stevens

The jailbait porn queen and the ultimate scream queen played beauty pageant contestants in Helix's "Gimme Gimme Good Lovin'" video. Two versions were filmed: In one they wore bikinis, in the other they went topless.

5. Susan Hatten

The hot blonde in Poison's "Fallen Angel."

6. Sharise Ruddell

Appeared in the Mötley Crüe video for "Girls Girls Girls." She married Vince Neil in 1988; they divorced in 1993.

7. Stephanie Seymour

Axl Rose's main squeeze–*cum*–punching bag appeared in the GNR videos "November Rain" and "Don't Cry."

8. Jennifer Gatti

She was the waifish runaway in Bon Jovi's "Runaway" video. She also played in *Star Trek: The Next Generation* and *The Young and the Restless*.

9. Lillian Mueller

The 1976 Playmate of the Year is the chemistry teacher who made Van Halen fans "Hot for Teacher."

10. Janet Jones

The future Mrs. Wayne Gretsky played Miss Phys Ed. in the same Van Halen clip.

A Fine Line Between Stupid and Clever: 11 Bands Whose "Controversial" Album Covers Were Banned, Censored, or Changed

1. Alice Cooper

The group's first album, *Pretties for You*, took its name from the cover painting, which shows a girl lifting up her dress to reveal her panties. It wasn't unusual for the few people who bought the record to find the panties covered with a sticker. The original cover for *Love It to Death* shows Alice holding his scarf in a way that makes his thumb look like a penis; some copies showed only half the cover, and some had the thumb airbrushed out. The Mexican release of the album *Killer* replaces the original picture of a snake, a sacred symbol in parts of Mexico, with something far less offensive: Alice hanging from a noose with blood pouring out of his mouth. The album *School's Out* also generated some controversy, but that time it was planned; after reading that it was illegal to import paper panties into America, it was decided that the inner sleeve holding the record would be a pair of paper panties.

2. Scorpions

Scorpions have gotten in trouble with several record covers as well. The release *Virgin Killer* is probably the most notorious, featuring a naked girl whose vagina is obscured by a cracked glass effect; it was replaced in several countries with a picture of the band. The half-naked breast on the cover of the band's *Love at First Sting* was also replaced this way, and so were the half-naked, caged women surrounded by tigers on the cover of *Pure Instinct*. *Lovedrive* features a man pulling a huge wad of gum from the breast of his female limousine companion. Women's groups were not pleased, and would later also make some noise over the cover of *Animal Magnetism*, which showed a woman kneeling in front of a man's crotch next to a large dog.

3. Guns N' Roses

The original cover of their debut album featured artist Robt. Williams' painting *Appetite for Destruction* until a scared Geffen Records moved it to the inside for American release and replaced it with the more familiar skulls-on-a-cross illustration. (Imported copies of the record featured the illustration on the front.) According to Williams, "When Guns N' Roses wanted to use my picture *Appetite for Destruction*, I told Axl he was going to get into trouble. Then they asked if they could use the title of the painting. I said yes, but I knew there'd be a problem. None of the guys in this band were too articulate, so they would direct the media to me to defend the cover."

4. Slayer

The bloody, nail-riddled Bible on the cover of *God Hates Us All* was replaced with four crosses on a white background.

5. Poison

When objections came about the cover for *Flesh and Blood* featuring a freshly inked tattoo, the offending, oozing blood was removed. After the release of *Open Up and Say… Ahh!* religious groups complained about the cover model Bambi being painted like a tiger and flashing her tongue like a snake. The picture was retouched so only Bambi's eyes are visible.

6. Brujeria

Some stores refused to stock *Matando Gueros* because the cover showed someone holding a very realistic-looking decapitated head.

7. Dimmu Borgir

The cloven-hoofed demon sitting tits to the wind on a throne surrounded by faceless people praying was banned in America and replaced with a slipcover that removed the tits, flames, and congregants.

8. Cradle of Filth

The graphic showing crucifixions and a woman holding a severed head in her lap replaced *Thornography*'s first cover: the woman wielding a bloody spike.

9. Bon Jovi

Slippery When Wet's original cover showed the charms of a big-titted babe in a wet T-shirt.

10. Marilyn Manson

Mechanical Animals featured a latex covered Manson with fake tits and no cock. When Wal-Mart complained, a version was created that placed the title over Mr. Manson's tits. They still wouldn't stock it.... Retailer Circuit City placed cardboard wrappers around the band's *Holy Wood (In the Valley of the Shadow of Death)* so all you can see is Manson's face, not the fact that he's being crucified.

11. Type O Negative

The original cover for the band's sophomore, faux-live album, *The Origin of the Feces*, showed what is allegedly Peter Steele's asshole. The replacement cover showed dancing skeletons from the painting *The Dance of Death*.

25 Band Names About . . . Well . . . You Figure It Out

1. Cockpit (an all-girl metal band)
2. GodCock
3. Satanic Cockrockers
4. Necrocock
5. Cock and Ball Torture
6. Cock-Knocker 666
7. Rotting Cock
8. Gag on My Cock
9. Purulent Spermcanal
10. Semen
11. Sperm of Mankind
12. Sperm Injection
13. Sucking Cock Castration
14. Sperma
15. Cum Laude

16. Spermswamp
17. Cumbeast
18. Cumgun
19. Goblin Cock
20. Here It Cums
21. The Cumshots
22. Bloodcum
23. Cum on Her Face
24. Creamface
25. Drowned in Cum

Hammers of the Gods: 28 Well-Hung Metalheads

The average penis size of the adult male human being is between five and six inches. According to Donna's Domain on the website Metal Sludge, these heavy metal musicians more than measure up.

1. Peter Steele (Type O Negative) — 11 inches
2. Derrick Green (Sepultura) — 8 inches
3. Chris Caffery (Savatage) — 7 inches
4. Tom Hamilton (Aerosmith) — 8 inches
5. Dez (Coal Chamber) — 7 inches
6. Bret Michaels (Poison) — 7 inches
7. Paul Stanley (Kiss) — 7 to 8 inches
8. Twiggy Ramirez (Marilyn Manson) — 8 inches
9. Jeff Hanneman (Slayer) — 7 to 8 inches
10. Tom Araya (Slayer) — 7 inches
11. Zack de la Rocha (Rage Against the Machine) — 9 inches
12. Phil Anselmo (Pantera) — 10 inches
13. Erik "A.K." Knutson (Flotsam & Jetsam) — 7 to 8 inches
14. Stet Howland (W.A.S.P.) — 7.5 inches
15. Tom Bettini (Jackyl) — 7.5 inches
16. Chad Gray (Mudvayne) — 8 inches
17. Rikki Rockett (Poison) — 9 inches
18. Ahrue Luster (Machine Head) — 8 inches
19. Viv Campbell (Def Leppard) — 7 inches
20. Riki Rachtman — 8 inches
21. Phil Varone (Skid Row) — 8 inches
22. Tracii Guns (L.A. Guns) — 8.5 inches
23. Fred Coury (Cinderella) — 8.5 to 9 inches
24. Joey Castillo (Danzig) — 10 inches
25. Dani Filth (Cradle of Filth) — 9 inches
26. Matt Sorum (Velvet Revolver) — 8 inches
27. Jason Hook (Vince Neil Band) — 9.5 inches
28. Jerry Cantrell (Alice in Chains) — 10 inches

Ken Susi of Unearth's Top 10 Spots to Fuck Groupies

1. In the balcony of an arena while watching Dimebag and Vinnie Paul jamming with Damageplan.
2. Behind a Dumpster at the venue. Dumpster sex! YEAH!
3. In the back lounge of the bus with your bandmates watching with hidden cameras.
4. In a groupie's sister's bed while the sister is at a sleepover. So creepy!
5. In a roadside jerk booth while people are watching through the glory holes.
6. In a room with all your band dudes trying to sleep around you.
7. In your bus while her boyfriend is outside waiting for her to come back with my autograph.
8. At a girl's apartment with her boyfriend sleeping in the other room.
9. In the ladies' room.
10. In an alley.

When not banging groupies in all sorts of weird places, Ken Susi plays guitar with Metal Blade recording artists Unearth and is the mastermind behind System Recordings.

Comedian and *That Metal Show* Co-Host Jim Florentine's 5 Motörhead Songs to Fuck Your Chick To

1. "Love Me Like a Reptile"
Self-explanatory.

2. "The Chase Is Better Than the Catch"
You probably spent a while trying to get in her pants. You finally got your catch. It's a four-minute song. Enjoy. I can go twice in that span.

3. "Jailbait"
I know what you're thinking. "I know she's only fourteen but she looks at least seventeen." Enjoy it before you go to prison and your ass gets pounded harder than the Gulf of Mexico during Hurricane Katrina.

4. "I'm So Bad Baby I Don't Care"
It lets her know that you'll come quicker than an obedient dog.

5. "No Class"

She'll know why you're fucking her in your backseat instead of getting a room.

Jim Florentine is best known as the voice of Special Ed on Comedy Central's Crank Yankers *and as the guy who spends his days turning the tables on* Telemarketers. *He has appeared on* The Apprentice, Down and Dirty with Jim Norton *on HBO, Comedy Central's* Mother Load, *HBO's* Inside the NFL, The Late Late Show with Craig Kilborn, *and many other shows. He can be seen co-hosting* That Metal Show *on VH1 Classic with Eddie Trunk and Don Jamieson.*

You've Got Another Thing Coming: 6 Openly Gay Metalheads

1. Rob Halford (Judas Priest)

Despite his very public taste for leather and studs, Halford's sexual orientation was a big surprise in some sections of the metal community. His decision to come out of the closet in 1998 raised a few eyebrows as well as the ire of some of his more closed-minded fans. Overall, though, he recalls the experience positively, telling one fan in an online interview, "The whole coming out experience for me was tremendously uplifting and satisfying, one that I shared with my fans around the world. The support and encouragement [I received] have gotten me through the difficult moments."

2. Otep Shamaya (Otep)

An outspoken sexual-abuse survivor, the tattooed blonde singer is currently the only out lesbian in metal, and she's just as likely to be seen in the gay press as the music press, thanks to her work for rape and incest survivor groups like RAINN. Speaking of how being gay has impacted her standing in the metal community, she told *Philadelphia Gay News*, "The fact that I find women beautiful doesn't have anything to do with the quality of our work or our songs. I think it would be more of an issue if I was a guy. One of the biggest stereotypes of people who are interested in same-gender relationships is that [people think] I can't find men attractive, which is absolutely false. I just don't have a sexual interest in them."

3. Doug Pinnick (King's X)

The bassist and singer for the Christian metallers came out in 1998 in an interview with *Re:generation Quarterly*; the band was dropped from its distribution deal with Diamante Music Group shortly thereafter. Asked about being a closeted homosexual,

Pinnick has said, "I've always been one to talk about the truth as I see it, no matter what it is. I felt like, if I'm going to preach about being honest [in my songs], I need to be honest, too. I didn't realize that I wasn't. I mean, it's been a very, very hard battle for me, being gay, because I'm homophobic. I was raised that way, so I hated myself. But when it started to get to me psychologically, I just had to come out of my closet and say, 'This is who I am. Love me or leave me.'"

4. Pink Stëël

A German heavy metal comedy act who combine gay culture with metal culture as they blow . . . your mind with songs like "Sausage Party" and "I'm Coming Out (All Over You)" from their albums *Creaming for Vengeance* and *Out at the Devil*. Founding band members Hanson Jobb and Udo Von DüYü say their mission is to "conquer the world, one bathhouse at a time."

5. Nanowar

This Italian metal band is a gay-themed takeoff on the band Manowar, and perform song parodies including "True Metal of Steel," "A Knight at the Opera," and "We Would Die for Metal Too, if We Made Money Like Manowar Do."

6. Gaahl (Gorgoroth)

The former singer for the black metal group Gorgoroth admitted to a "close relationship" with modeling agent Dan DeVero, which began after the two worked together on a video shoot. The pair are no longer involved romantically, but started a women's clothing company together. "Those who know me in private didn't think it was particularly strange," Gaahl says. "I do not care about what people in general think. . . . Besides, I like confusing people."

70 X-Rated Band Names

1. Mincing Fury and Guttural Clamour of Queer Decay
2. Porno Maniak 100% Syphilis Addiction
3. Bestially Raped Till Dismembered
4. Catasexual Urge Motivation
5. Nunwhore Commando 666
6. Nasty Nympho Chocolate
7. Sodomizing Pornogenerator
8. Tentacle Pornmonster
9. Fistfuck
10. Fuck on the Beach
11. Fucksaw
12. Corpsefucking Art
13. Funeral Rape
14. Flesh Parade
15. Fetish

16. Bizarre Bondage
17. A Concubine's Diary
18. Bitch Hunter
19. Whore
20. Putrid Whore
21. Whorifik
22. Obsceno
23. Carnal
24. Carnal Diafragma
25. Brutal Nekkro Sex
26. Cemetery Rapist
27. Copremesis
28. Feto in Fetus
29. For You Dear Pederast
30. Pedofilia
31. Children of the Porn
32. Porno Infantil
33. Sheepfucker
34. Pisshitter
35. Shemale
36. Immaculate Molestation
37. Bitch Infection
38. Gonorrhoeaction
39. Venereal Messiah
40. Rotten Penetration
41. Gorgasm
42. Kastrated
43. Prostitute Disfigurement
44. Psychosadistic Haterapist
45. Sexgrind Morbidus
46. Libido Airbag
47. Sex Diaries
48. Sikfuk
49. Torso Fuck
50. Death Fuck
51. The Fuck Machine
52. The Meatfuckers
53. Vilefuck
54. Sexfuck
55. Skullfuck
56. Necrofuckinglicious
57. Ready to Fuck
58. Tankfucker
59. Funeral Fuck
60. Fucktotum
61. Fuck Your Shadow from Behind
62. Nofuck
63. Cluster Fuck
64. Bullfuck
65. Go Get Fucked
66. Celtic Buttfuck
67. F.U.C.Kings
68. Fuck Inc.
69. FuckThis
70. Fuck You All

3 Heavy Metal Performers Arrested for Sex Crimes

1. Gene Simmons (Kiss)

The Demon was arrested backstage in Columbus, Georgia, on charges of indecent exposure during the band's *Crazy Nights* tour. According to Simmons, Gene Jr. had become a little uncomfortable while sleeping in his Spandex banana hammock, so Papa Gene ran to the side of the stage to adjust his nuts and get back to the gig. Gene says he was under arrest for about an hour and then released.

2. Marilyn Manson

The former rock journalist Brian Warner was sued for sexual assault and intentional infliction of emotional distress after rubbing his leather-thonged crotch and panty-hosed thighs back and forth . . . again and again . . . on a security guard's head during a gig in Detroit. Both parties reached an agreement and the charges were dropped. Mr. Manson has been arrested or warned about indecent exposure several times, too. Jacksonville, Florida, police arrested Manson for indecent exposure in 1994 after he allegedly whipped it out onstage, although he might have been wearing a strap-on at the time. He was arrested on the same charge in Rome because of his ass-revealing outfits, and was told not to wear the same costumes in several other Italian towns. He wore them anyway.

3. Wendy O. Williams (Plasmatics)

From the second Plasmatics hit the stage, theirs was one of the most sex-drenched gigs going. She was arrested—and acquitted—in Milwaukee and Cleveland for onstage obscenity, specifically simulating sex with a sledgehammer. She was also charged in Cleveland for doing this while wearing shaving cream on her tits.

Dr. Dot's 8 Heavy Metal Hardbodies

Better known as the Masseuse to the Stars, Dr. Dot helps celebrities around the world stretch their muscles, relax their bodies, and get their kinks out—and no, she's not that kind of masseuse, so don't even ask her for a happy ending. Here are some of her favorite heavy metal clients.

1. Peter Steele (Type O Negative)

If you dig deep enough, you'll find nude pictures of Peter online, so you don't have to take my word for it when I say his body is to die for. Aside from being almost seven feet tall, he's built like a brick shithouse. His deep voice, piercing light eyes, and dark hair make him one of my favorite clients. I'm always in the mood to massage him!

2. Gene Simmons (Kiss)

Gene makes my list because he's fit in all the right places, especially his buns of steel. Gene says I gave him his first massage ever. He never likes to lose control—which has to happen during a massage—so it took a while to convince him to relax. Gene's ambition and success are an inspiration to me and the fact that he doesn't drink or do drugs, is a great father, and has a wild sense of humor make him super fun to be

around. Some say he has a big ego, but I say he deserves to have a big ego. Everything he touches turns to gold.

3. Robert Plant (Led Zeppelin)

I first met Robert when I was seventeen years old. Robert loves my massages and my hands love Robert. His whole body is so masculine and firm, especially his legs (must be from all the tennis playing and running away from adoring, horny females). Getting paid to massage such a man feels insane. Most would pay to massage him. I feel grateful to have stretched his lean muscles. What a whole lotta love.

4. Steven Tyler (Aerosmith)

Steven is so much fun to massage. He's fit as fuck, sexy but not in-your-face sexy. The man just can't help it. Plus he's funny as hell. One time I was massaging Steven's voluptuous lips and I told him, "I call this the Mick Jagger Method." He said, "Wait! Look at my lips. Aren't my lips bigger than Mick's?" He opened his mouth as wide as he could and then closed it and made a "brrrrrrrr" sound. I said, "You know, your lips are bigger!" He said, "You can call that the Steven Tyler Method now."

5. Lemmy Kilmister (Motörhead)

Just because Lemmy doesn't flaunt his body doesn't mean he isn't packing heat. The funny thing is, I'd been massaging Motörhead for a couple years but never got to do Lemmy. He always said, "I don't like to relax. I enjoy the tension." One time he was telling me about how much he hates massage, I started giving his hands a deep-tissue massage. He didn't even notice and kept on talking about how irritating massages must be. Then I rolled up his sleeve and did his arm. Still talking, he helped by taking off his shirt. I massaged his muscular back while he spoke about how he doesn't see the point in relaxing. Before he knew it, he had his first massage. And he enjoyed it.

6. Dave Mustaine (Megadeth)

Some people whine about Dave and his ego, but he can back up that self-confidence with his playing, his slammin', unmarked body, and his gorgeous face. During one massage, I was thinking to myself, "Wow, what a body!" Towards the end I told him, "Dave, you're the first rocker I've massaged who doesn't have a single tattoo." He grinned and said, "Baby, you don't put a bumper sticker on a Cadillac!"

7. Dave Navarro (Jane's Addiction, Red Hot Chili Peppers)

Dave's body oozes sexuality. I'm pretty sure if you looked up "Heavy Metal Hardbody" in the dictionary, you'd see this cocky motherfucker's picture. I massaged him when he played with the Chili Peppers and he loved it so much, he got one before and after the show. He also got so much attention and massage from me that no one else got a chance. Sorry, Flea!

8. Steve Vai

Steve is as hot as he is unique, confident, and talented. The man is 100 percent dedicated to his lucky wife and still has a body that screams, "Ride me." Let me just say Steve makes my job difficult, but not on purpose. I find it hard to think pure, wholesome thoughts while massaging one of the world's sexiest (and sweetest) rockers.

Dr. Dot is a self-described "rock chick" who wanted to meet her musical heroes without exchanging sexual favors. To get backstage she would perform massages, which she'd been perfecting since she was five years old. She wrote about her experiences massaging the biggest and best names in rock in the book Butt Naked and Backstage. *She has been profiled in numerous magazines and television shows.*

Your Time Is Gonna Come: 20 Bands Singing the Praises of Necrophilia

1. Gorelord
"Necrophilic Orgy in Entrails & Cum"
"Alive When Fucking the Dead"

2. Dark Angel
"An Ancient Inherited Shame"

3. Cannibal Corpse
"Worm Infested"

4. Devourment
"Fuck Her Head Off"

5. Alice Cooper
"I Love the Dead"
"Cold Ethyl"

6. Rigor Sardonicus
"Homophile Necrophilia"

7. Savatage
"Necrophilia"

8. Face Down
"The Will to Power"

9. Fleshgrind
"Organ Harvest"

10. The Candles Burning Blue
"How the Black Art Was Revealed"

11. Cattle Decapitation
"Land of the Severed Meatus"

12. Gorgasm
"Stabwound Intercourse"

13. Pathologist
"Cannibalistic Disfigurement"

14. Impetigo
"I Work for the Street Cleaner"

15. Putrid Pile
"Covered in Excrement"

16. Tormentor
"Tormentor 1"

17. Moral Decay
"Beyond Forensic Knowledge"

18. Cradle of Filth
"Lord Abortion"

19. Misteria
"Paradise of Madmen"

20. Slayer
"Necrophiliac"

21 BAND NAMES ABOUT ... ASS!

1. Assück
2. Anal Whore
3. Anal Orgasm
4. First Test of Anal Shit
5. Anal Blast
6. Orbital Anal Blast
7. Rotten Rectum
8. Anal Cunt
9. Hemorragia Anal
10. Anal Nosorog
11. Hemorrhoidal Anal Suffering
12. Anal Penetration
13. Anal Massaker
14. Ass Universe
15. GoreAnus
16. Anal Gore Terror
17. Insane Assholes
18. Anal Terror of the Megacocks
19. MortAnus
20. Urtikaria Anal
21. Anal Trauma

5 Porn Stars with Metal-Inspired Stage Names . . .

1. Ava Vincent
The former Jewel Valmont renamed herself midcareer, taking Vince Neil's first name for her last.

2. Ava Lee Roth
The curvy brunette star of pornos including *Screamin' for Semen*, *No Holes Left Unfilled*, and *Fuck Me First* is, according to legend, David Lee Roth's daughter. Diamond Dave has neither confirmed nor denied the claim.

3. Sikki Nixx
The heavily inked Nixx appeared in forty porn movies, including *Edward Penishands*, *Zane's World*, and *Headbangers Ball*. He was once married to porn star Jeanna Fine.

4. Nikki Sexx
Sexx is featured in such flicks as *Slutty and Sluttier 8* and *Cream Plosions 3*.

5. Allysin Chaynes
The namesake of Jerry Cantrell's heavy metal/ hard rock hybrid has been in over three hundred movies, including *Backstage Slut* and *Sex, Drugs and Rock-n-Roll*.

. . . and One Metal Band That Returned the Favor

Alexisonfire
The band named itself after lactating contortionist porn star stripper Alexis Fire.

Director Matt Zane of Society 1 Remembers 25 Metalheads Who Appeared in His Porn Movies

Pornographer Matt Zane pioneered the "alt-porn" genre back in the '90s, when he scored several hits with his *Backstage Sluts* video line. The videos featured hard-core sex acts, live musical performances, band interviews, and porn stars being thwacked with slices of lunch meat. These are some of the folks who lived *that much more* of the rock 'n' roll dream.

1. Jonathan Davis (Korn)

This interview was interesting because it was done before Jonathan really admitted he was into porn. A few years later he ended up marrying a porn star.

2. Insane Clown Posse

These guys were very much into the idea of groupies, and they were the first band we had throw lunch meat at a naked porn starlet. One of the actresses gave Violent J a blow job after the shoot.

3. Fred Durst and Wes Borland (Limp Bizkit)

Fred agreed to be filmed, but for some reason he wanted an alter ego named "Vinnie the Weapon." Sporting a bad mustache and Afro, he molested a porn chick and she loved it. He even let her stick her hand down his pants and stroke him off on film. Wes was also doing the whole alter ego thing, but his character wasn't as developed.

4. Nashville Pussy

I just remember being surprised the band had the word *pussy* in their name!

5. Jay Gordon (Orgy)

I shot the scene with Jay before his first record was out. He looked like he'd be famous, so I figured what the hell. After all these years we actually remain friends.

6. Lynn Strait (Snot)

Lynn did a full-blown sex scene with his girlfriend and a porn chick for one of my movies. This was actually the first time a porn film featured a "rock star" fucking. He was a trailblazer, before Tommy Lee or Evan Seinfeld.

7. Lemmy Kilmister (Motörhead)

This was tough interview to shoot because there are swastikas all over his apartment. We kept trying to frame the shot so you wouldn't see any Nazi memorabilia, but it was next to impossible. If you look in the mirror in one shot you can see a corner of a Nazi flag.

8. Twiggy Ramirez (Marilyn Manson, NIN, Perfect Circle)

Twiggy told me he was trying to clean up his image before the interview. Then he told me about wrapping a girl with meat and urinating on her.

9. Ben Moody (Evanescence)

I couldn't believe he agreed to appear in one of my movies. I shot him during a Kelly Clarkson session he was producing.

10. Markku (Hoobastank)

The only reason I was able to get Markku was because we used to be in a band together. I actually kicked him out; then he started Hoobastank and now lives in a mansion with an elevator.

11. Papa Roach

I told them that if they were in my movie their first record would go platinum. It actually sold multiplatinum. Years later they still remember that conversation.

12. Genitorturers

I was surprised that Gen agreed to do an interview with me. I almost ran their bus off the road on tour one year, and later, at an event my band was playing with them, their bus driver pulled a gun on my bassist because he thought he was the one driving.

13. Eve 6

They were another band I talked into throwing lunch meat at a porn girl.

14. Crowbar

They're nice guys. After the show and interview we went back to my place. I sent Kirk into a room with a chick who I undressed for him to fuck. Their guitar player at the time told me about how he loved fucking corpses in a morgue.

15. Pimpadelic

During the shoot there was a scene where the lead singer was supposed to snort blow off a chick's ass. He actually brought real blow. After he did the take I had to explain to him that we had to reshoot it a few times.

16. Zebrahead

That was a good piano player. Wanted to wear fake teeth for some reason.

17. Jason Miller (Godhead)

I was surprised Jason agreed to be in my movie, but then again, it was before he toured with me!

18. Adrian Ost (Powerman 5000)

He had trouble staying focused on the story because a naked porn chick named Tabitha Stevens was letting him fondle her tits.

19. Mike Ransom (Adema)

He was sitting next to Adrian and didn't say much. Then again, he had the bottom half of a naked Tabitha Stevens.

20. Wolfpack

These guys always sent me footage and would include the tits and booze. They even included the release forms! They have their debauchery down to a science.

21. Dope

I shot an additional scene with Edsel and Racy besides the one in the final cut that for some reason never surfaced. During the scene Edsel wanted to put chocolate syrup over this chick's ass and lick it off. I kept telling him no and he didn't understand why. After the shoot he was kind of pissed until I explained that on-camera it would have looked like he was eating the chick's shit.

22. Preston Na$h (Primer 55, Society 1)

The fact that he banged a midget puts him in another level than most in my movies.

23. Dirt (Society 1)

After the first show he played on tour with Society 1, he somehow filmed me fisting a chick. That always seems to be a memory he recalls fondly when asked about his early career.

24. Ill Niño

This was interesting because in the middle of the interview Laz admitted he was genuinely excited that I was filming him for one of my flicks.

25. In This Moment

I don't think they knew they were being filmed for a porno!

At one time the youngest adult video director in history, Matt Zane lays first claim to mixing rock and porn with his series Backstage Sluts. *After releasing albums with his band Society 1, Zane became the first vocalist to sing while suspended and broke the world record for most-attended suspension at Download Festival 2005. He sang for thirty-five minutes with four hooks. He's the first person to perform a guitar solo while suspended. In January 2008, Zane broke the world record for longest body suspension—previously held by Criss Angel—by hanging from four hooks for six hours.*

4 Heavy Metal Non-Sex Porn Film Cameos

1. Lemmy Kilmister (Motörhead)

Lemmy appears in *John Wayne Bobbitt: Uncut*, starring the ex-Marine whose wife cut his penis off after an alleged spousal rape. Lemmy appears sitting on a park bench when Lorena (Veronica Brazil) tosses her husband's severed cock out of a car window. It lands at Lemmy's feet. He looks down at John's willy and says, "Looks like a dick!"

2. Vince Neil (Mötley Crüe)

Neil also appears in *John Wayne Bobbitt: Uncut*, playing a bartender.

3. Ted Nugent

Ted's here more in spirit than anything else. A scene in *Gutter Mouths 17* starts off with two guys (Dave Hardman and Backey Jakic) and a girl (Briana Banks) excitedly talking about seeing the Motor City Madman in concert that night. When Hardman leaves to pick up the tickets, Briana tries to pick up Jakic by saying, "I love Ted Nugent. He really turns me on!" Hardman returns to find the pair doing the wango tango and whips it out. Briana giggles, "The only thing I like more than Ted Nugent is a hard cock!" then gets down to business on Hardman's cock. After the pair do their business on her face, Hardman picks Briana off the floor and says, "Now get your come-drenched ass dressed so we can go see the fuckin' Nuge!"

4. Dave Navarro (Jane's Addiction, Red Hot Chili Peppers)

Navarro made his first excursion into full-length filmmaking with the porn flick *Broken* starring Sasha Grey. Navarro gets a decent amount of screen time himself, playing the director of a porn flick.

Jasmin St. Claire's 10 Reasons Metal Dudes Are So Hot . . .

1. The sweat that drips off them when they play metal, bang their heads (no pun intended), or come out of a mosh pit. I love it when a guy sweats all over me!
2. Long hair. I love running my fingers through a guy's hair and grabbing onto it during sex!

3. They have great taste in music, obviously!
4. Tattoos. A guy can never have too many tattoos. They represent so much about a person and look so sexy, especially if a guy has long hair hanging down his back, covering them up a little.
5. Living the heavy metal lifestyle is a big turn-on.
6. Metalheads are the best lovers! They make me want more and more!
7. They have aggressive attitudes.
8. Headbanging is so sexy!
9. Their clothes! I love a guy in camouflage pants or dressed all in black. It makes me want to do very naughty things!
10. I love nerds, and most metal men are nerds deep down inside.

. . . and 10 Reasons Why Metal Chicks Are So Hot

1. We rate an 11 instead of a 10 because we're just that much hotter for loving metal and metalhead guys!
2. Ya never mess with a true metal chick. We can throw down like no one else!
3. Short skirts, knee-high boots, tight pants, and studded bracelets!
4. We like our sex like we like our music: pounding, hard, and loud!
5. A metal chick tells it like it is, and we don't take anyone's crap.
6. Metal chicks are hard to find. How many women are there who truly love metal? You tell me how many chicks you see at a metal show.
7. A metal dude can talk shop with a metal chick and she'll know what he's talking about.
8. Dark eye makeup is super sexy and mysterious.
9. We always support our bands, and we're loyal as hell to our men.
10. Who else understands a metal dude better than a metal chick? Trust me, no suit-wearing preppy priss could understand a metal man! Metal chicks understand their men and their lifestyle!

Jasmin St. Claire was involved in the ECW wrestling circuit from 1999 to 2001 and took part in ownership of a wrestling company from 2002 to 2004. A natural at bringing the brutal truth to the masses, Jasmin has hosted several metal events and programs since 1998, including the Milwaukee Metalfest, the documentary Hollywood Rocks, *and the TV show* Metal Scene. *She also writes for publications such as* Rock City News, Rock Brigade, *and* Hard Rocker *and hosts Brazil's premier heavy metal TV show, Stay Heavy TV.*

Whole Lotta Continua: Sasha Grey's 16 Favorite Metal Albums 'n' Shit

This is it, as far as I'm concerned—that whole "desert island disc" thing. I just want to know where the hell you're supposed to get the electricity on a deserted island!

1. *Masters of Reality*—Black Sabbath

Of course this is going to be at the top of my list, just as it is at the top of many. I mean really, the opening to "Lord of this World" is dope shit. I'd sacrifice a whole bunch of lame Republicans to see Sabbath live in their prime. This album represents a stunning document that has no true equal.

2. *Screaming for Vengeance*—Judas Priest

The archetypal Priest album in the eyes of many. Fronted by the metal god Rob Halford, Priest have been one of the defining bands of the metal movement. "You've Got Another Thing Coming" helped to create a new generation of metalheads and showed the world that metal rules!

3. *Number of the Beast*—Iron Maiden

Winning fans from all areas of the metal spectrum, Iron Maiden clearly are one of the true innovators in heavy metal. The intro to the track "Number of the Beast" has become one of the "prayers" of heavy metal, with just about every fan knowing it word for word.

4. *No Remorse*—Motörhead

It's fucking Lemmy! I have a German friend who loves Motörhead. One time he shared a drink with Lemmy at some crazy bar in Munich and they both puked up rust. Yes, I said rust. That's pretty fucking metal. Besides, you *know* Lemmy can eat good pussy!

5. Sleep

I don't understand why they call this stoner metal. Does it really matter what album? I mean, ever since that scene in *Gummo* where they play Dragonaut and the kids are all . . . Wait . . . What was I talking about . . . ? Wait, it'll come to me. . . .

6. Nyogthaeblisz

Black metal. Again, it doesn't matter what the album title is, because you won't be able to find it anyway. The 7-inch came with a razor blade. Go fuck yourself—that's my name.

7. *November Coming Fire*—Samhain

I've been to Lodi, New Jersey . . . during the p.m., but I've been . . . so I can begin to understand were Glenn gets his . . . uh . . . motivation. I'd want to get the fuck out of Lodi, too. "To walk the night" . . . Not really Misfits and not yet the Danzig we all know—more of an atmospheric and dirty sound.

8. *Blizzard of Ozz*—Ozzy Osbourne

Oh, the exquisite carnality of it all. Not only does this album provide some of Ozzy's most notable tracks, but the mystique and influence of this record have truly stood the test of time.

9. *Undertow*—Tool

MJK's voice is so dynamic it's scary. This album is all about how if you eat bad jelly beans enough you will begin to see little men trapped underneath the floor running around in a heated isolated depression. It's important really to understand that this is the theme of the whole album. Beans. It's all about them beans, man.

10. *Weight*—Rollins Band

Would you piss this guy off? Hell, no! Rollins isn't just punk rock anymore. With a set of sick complex grooves and old Hank looking like his head will explode at any moment, this album was pretty fucking crazy when it came out in the early '90s.

11. *Seasons in the Abyss*—Slayer

Ah, Slayer, mmmm. Slayer, in my mind, are the incontrovertible speed metal kings. *Seasons in the Abyss* showed Slayer at its most refined point, with a mix of both groove-oriented and speed metal thrash tracks. By far the most popular Slayer album to date, and for good reason. Best tracks are "War Ensemble," "Spirit in Black," "Dead Skin Mask," and of course "Seasons in the Abyss."

12. *. . .And Justice for All*—Metallica

I know, I know. The bass is mixed to almost nothing, and Jason was no Cliff Burton. But "Blackened" and the title track are pretty epic. . . . Not to mention that "One" song—what was it called?

13. *IX Equilibrium*—Emperor

Arson, murder, and perpetual performance art. If you don't know it, you need to.

14. *How the Gods Kill*—Danzig

Produced by the bearded wonder Rick Rubin. The third time around is perfect for that bluesy, sweaty, punched-in-the-gut-by-way-of-the-asshole feeling. Danzig knows how to pull you in romantically, and then fuck the shit out of you without making you feel guilty. This album is like the lost sound track to a road movie where kooky kids get lost in the bayou and then get fucked up, *Deliverance* style.

15. *Killing Is My Business and Business Is Good*—Megadeth
Did you ever see the *Behind the Music* episode about Dave Mustaine and Megadeth? Oh my fucking Christ! This cat's truly had nine lives and has maintained his relevance where most of his contemporaries have been watered down. He's always kept true to his ideals, whether political or artistic.

16. *World Turns on Its Hinge*—Ash Pool
What, you've never heard of them? Bullshit. . . Why not?

Star of more than eighty porn films, Sasha Grey was featured in the November 2006 edition of Los Angeles *magazine, which flagged her as a potential major star, the next Jenna Jameson. Grey was also* Penthouse *Pet of the Month for July 2007, photographed by the fashion photographer Terry Richardson. In 2008, she won female performer of the year at the 25th Annual AVN Awards. She is also featured in the artwork for the Smashing Pumpkins album* Zeitgeist, *has modeled for American Apparel and Richard Kern for* Vice *magazine, starred in Steven Soderbergh's* The Girlfriend Experience, *and made the 2009* Rolling Stone *Hot List.*

NOISE

19 Unlikely Heavy Metal Pairings (and One Honorable Mention)

1. Alice Cooper and Liza Minnelli

Liza sang background vocals on the 1974 album *Muscle of Love*; so did the Pointer Sisters and Ronnie Spector.

2. Liza Minnelli and ensemble

Liza joined in on "We Are the Champions" as part of the big finale at the 1992 Freddie Mercury Tribute Concert.

3. Elton John and Axl Rose

The pair performed "Bohemian Rhapsody" with Queen at the Freddie Mercury Tribute Concert.

4. Tony Iommi and Jethro Tull

Iommi was a member of Tull very briefly in 1969 and only "played" with Tull once: when they appeared in *The Rolling Stones: Rock and Roll Circus*, miming "Song for Jeffrey."

5. Lou Reed and Kiss

New York's rock poet laureate contributed the songs "Dark Light," "A World Without Heroes" and "Mr. Blackwell" to *Music from the Elder*.

6. Kiss and Desmond Child

Disco sucks. Unless you can get a hot producer to crank out a hit like "I Was Made For Loving You." Child is a longtime friend of Paul Stanley's, and they continue to collaborate.

7. Peter Criss and Gene Krupa

The Kiss Catman took drum lessons from the jazz great when he was a teen.

8. Paul Stanley and Sarah Brightman

The Starchild sings with Brightman on "I Will Be with You (Where the Lost Ones Go)" from the pop soprano's CD *Symphony*.

9. Eric Adams and Sarah Brightman

Brightman and Manowar frontman Adams collaborated on the beautiful ballad "Where Eagles Fly." The song was circulated on an EP before the release of Brightman's *Harem*, but was left off the final disc and remains unreleased.

10. Ian Gillan and Luciano Pavarotti

Shortly before Pavarotti's death, the pair sang together on Pavarotti's signature song, "Nessun Dorma."

11. Ozzy Osbourne and Mariah Carey

Concerts on Mariah Carey's 1999 *Rainbows* tour opened with a video chronicling the rivalry between the diva and her bad-girl alter ego, Bianca. Some of the people confessing their fave of the two are Naomi Campbell, Donny and Marie, and Ozzy Osbourne, who liked Bianca best.

12. Aerosmith and Fergie

The band performed "Walk This Way" with Fergie at Fashion Rocks in 2007.

13. Aerosmith and Britney Spears, Mary J. Blige and 'NSync

The pop powerhouses performed "Walk This Way" during the Super Bowl XXXV half-time show.

14. Jimmy Page and Johnny Thunders (kinda)

Page once sent a car around to pick Thunders up so the pair could jam together. Thunders declined the offer because of, uh, poor health.

15. Eddie Van Halen and Michael Jackson

Van Halen played the solo in the song "Beat It" in 1983, making it one of the first—if not *the* first—heavy metal/R&B hybrids. Slash performed the song on TV with Jackson during the Jacksons' Thirtieth Anniversary Special.

16. Tommy Lee and Lil' Kim

Lil' Kim appeared on Tommy's trip-hop/metal CD *Methods of Mayhem*.

17. Ozzy Osbourne and Busta Rhymes

Ozzy appeared on the track "Iron Man (This Is War)" from Busta's 1998 *CD Extinction Level Event (The Final World Front)*.

18. Def Leppard and Tim McGraw

Pop metal and pop country collide in the song "Nine Lives."

19. Alice Cooper and Glen Campbell

They dueted together at Alice's annual Christmas Pudding concert in Phoenix, Arizona, in 2004. Ted Nugent played guitar as well.

Honorable Mention

Tipper Gore and Diva Zappa

Former drummer Tipper plays along with Diva Zappa's song "When the Ball Drops" on the *Frank Zappa Aaafnraa Birthday Bundle* tribute record.

Gonna Make Your Ears Bleed: The World's 3 Loudest Heavy Metal Bands

3. Deep Purple

The 1975–1976 edition of the *Guinness Book of World Records* listed DP as hitting 117 dB.

2. Iron Maiden

At their 1988 Monsters of Rock gig, the band cranked out 124 dB, measured at the mixing tower. Other bands were hitting 118 dB.

1. Manowar

The Kings of Metal title was well earned when the *Guinness Book of Records* cited the band for "loudest musical performance" in 1984. They were again noted for the sheer, overwhelming loudness of it all when the *Guinness* folks declared them "the Loudest Band in the World" after a 129.5 dB performance in Hanover, Germany, in 1994. Although it wouldn't be "official" (the *Guinness Book* no longer acknowledges records for concert volume so they don't encourage hearing damage), the band outdid themselves (again) when they were measured at139 dB during their show at the Magic Circle Fest in Bad Arolsen, Germany, in 2008.

John 5 of Marilyn Manson's Top 10 Favorite Concerts and Tours of All Time

1. The Rolling Stones' *Tattoo You* tour 1981, Pontiac Silverdome, Pontiac, Michigan. This was my first concert.
2. Van Halen's 1984 tour
3. Nine Inch Nails' *Downward Spiral* tour
4. Iron Maiden's *Powerslave* tour
5. Oasis's *(What's the Story) Morning Glory* tour, Manchester, England
6. Iggy Pop's 1981 tour
7. Metallica's *Master of Puppets* tour, with Cliff Burton
8. Kiss's *Psycho Circus* tour
9. Slayer's *Reign in Blood* tour
10. The Eagles' New Year's Eve Millennium concert

Born John Lowery in Grosse Point, Michigan, John 5 started playing guitar at the age of seven, inspired by Saturday morning TV show Hee Haw: *"I didn't know any . . . musical genres. I was just in awe of the players." A session guitarist since the age of eighteen, John has worked on TV shows, commercials, and film sound tracks; toured with Lita Ford and kd lang; recorded with David Lee Roth and Rob Halford; and was a member of Marilyn Manson from 1998 to 2003; he currently plays alongside Rob Zombie. His latest release is* Remixploitation.

Unusual Versions of Led Zeppelin Songs Performed Live by Ex-Members

1. Jimmy Page

One of Page's first public performances after the demise of Led Zeppelin was an instrumental performance of "Stairway to Heaven" at Ronnie Lane's ARMS Benefit shows. Page also joined the later ARMS tour. Pagey and rapper Puff Daddy recorded their own version of "Kashmir" for the sound track of *Godzilla*, then performed it on *Saturday Night Live*. Jimmy and Leona Lewis performed "Whole Lotta Love" together to announce the 2010 Summer Olympic Games in London.

2. Robert Plant

Although there were no Zeppelin songs on their bluegrass album *Raising Sand*, Plant and Alison Krauss performed several Zep classics during their tour, including "Black Dog," "The Battle of Evermore," "When the Levee Breaks," and "Black Country Woman," which Zeppelin had never performed in concert themselves.

3. John Paul Jones

Jonesy has done Zeppelin songs with a diverse group of musicians. The encore for his tour with goth singer Diamanda Galás was usually "Communication Breakdown." He's performed "Going To California" with Warren Haynes and played "I Can't Quit You Baby" with jam band Government Mule. And a set with Ben Harper and ?uestlove at Bonnaroo in 2007 included "When the Levee Breaks," "Good Times, Bad Times," and a half-hour version of "Dazed and Confused."

Welcome to My Nightmare: Eric Danville's 5 Most Wanted Metal Bootlegs

I'm an unapologetic bootleg collector, with more than two thousand boots under my belt (and under my bed and under my sink). I've taped some shows myself; others I've bought, begged, borrowed, stolen, traded, or downloaded. I have plenty of shows I saw, but some of the metal gigs I've hit have escaped me. Here's your chance to hook a brother up. Get me these shows!

1. Black Sabbath/Van Halen—Madison Square Garden, New York, New York; August 27, 1978

I *must* have this show. Now. The crowd was off the hook. People burned crosses in the nosebleeds, and a big wooden cross from the floor section even made it onto the stage. The guy next to me pulled out a huge bag of weed and offered me some (I turned him down because my parents were going to pick me up afterwards), and there was a really hot chick wearing a cape a few rows in front of me with a black "666" written on her forehead and black triangles under her eyes. If I remember, the set list was great and they did all of *Paranoid* except "Hand of Doom." I don't know. I was fucking fifteen. And yeah, everything you've heard about Van Halen blowing Sabbath off the stage during this tour was true.

2. Judas Priest/Alice Cooper/Motörhead—Brendan Byrne Arena, East Rutherford, New Jersey; August 9, 1991

This gig from the *Operation Rock 'n' Roll* tour was full of firsts: My first time seeing Motörhead. My first time seeing Alice do the "jumping off the video screen" effect. My first time seeing Judas Priest. Motörhead was really fucking loud, even for an arena. It was also the first time I saw one of the Cycle Sluts from Hell in person, coming out of the bathroom.

3. Alice Cooper—Palladium, New York, New York; August 16, 1980

When I was eleven or twelve my mother told me I could listen to any of my brother's albums—except *Kick Out the Jams* by the MC5 and Cooper's *Love It to Death*. So of course the first thing I did when I was alone? Pull out *Love It to Death*, which I still listen to frequently. I didn't see Alice until I was old enough to go on my own, and this was it, with Mike Pinera of Iron Butterfly on guitar.

4. Twisted Sister—Fountain Casino, Aberdeen, New Jersey; August 31, 1981

The Fountain Casino was a beautifully cheesy rock club on the outskirts of Matawan, New Jersey, but for a while got some really great bands (I saw Cooper here a short while after the Palladium show). This was one of the band's SMF parties. They were as rocking as you've heard. The band was so loud my ears rang the whole next day. It was killer.

5. Guns N' Roses/Metallica/Faith No More—Giants Stadium, East Rutherford, New Jersey; July 18, 1992

A nice gig on a nice day, and the only time I got to see Guns. This wasn't the show where Axl got hit in the balls with a lighter. Unfortunately.

Eric Danville is the author of The Official Heavy Metal Book of Lists. *He prefers to ftp flacs, but MP3s are okay in a pinch.*

11 "Real" Musicians Who Have Played with Spinal Tap

1. Les Paul
2. Jeff Beck
3. Slash
4. Warren Haynes
5. Dweezil Zappa
6. Joe Satriani
7. Tim Renwick
8. Steve Lukather
9. David Gilmour
10. Pino Palladino
11. Mick Fleetwood

Give the Drummer Some: 6 Outrageous Drum Solo Stunts

1. Neal Smith (Alice Cooper)

In the late '60s and early '70s, it wasn't unusual for the tall and lanky drummer to start his solo, throw his sticks away, then play the drums with his hands. He'd then get up from behind the kit, walk to the front of it—still playing with his hands—then start punching and kicking the shit out of it until he fell over or a band member pulled him away.

2. John Bonham (Led Zeppelin)

John Bonham's drum solos during "Pat's Delight" and "Moby Dick" are the stuff of legend, eventually becoming marathons that clocked in at over thirty minutes (according to the band's website, Bonzo's longest solo was during the band's April 1977 show in Dallas, Texas). He originally avoided visual gimmickry like smoke or lasers in favor of the music, but during Zep's '73 tour, the end of "Moby Dick" was signaled by Bonham thrashing a huge flaming gong; the effect was captured for posterity in *The Song Remains the Same*. Bonham also lays claim to being the first rock drummer to use hydraulic drum risers, which moved him forward on the stage, and during his solos he'd use phasers and synthesizers on the drums to keep it interesting. Bonzo outdid himself during his thirty-first birthday show at the Los Angeles Forum, when "Moby Dick" featured maybe the most special effect of all: his buddy Keith Moon, who played timpani.

3. Peter Criss (Kiss)

Between Gene Simmons's fire-breathing, Ace Frehley's smoking guitar, and Paul Stanley's chest hair, the Catman could get lost in the background during a Kiss show—until it came time for his drum solo. His drum kit would rise twenty to thirty feet in the air as sparks flew, lights spun, and flash pots went off, two cats sitting at either side keeping watch with glowing eyes.

4. Alex Van Halen (Van Halen)

How many members of Van Halen does it take to do a drum solo? Four, if you saw the band play back in the late '70s. Alex would start beating his skins and the other members of the band would each pick up some sticks and start playing cymbals or a tom-tom. A strobe light flashed in time with the drums too, until the strobe eventually became a steady stream of light. That was *really cool* when you were fifteen years old.

5. Tommy Lee (Mötley Crüe)

Tommy Lee's brand of heavy metal excess didn't just take place offstage; his drum solos included some typically over-the-top gimmicks and effects. On some tours Lee's drum kit would rise, tilt from side to side, and spin 360 degrees till he looked like a hamster in a spinning wheel. On some tours he would fly, attached to a harness, up to the ceiling, where he would play his solo before coming back down to earth. As his taste grew to include an appreciation for hip-hop, Lee also had drum loops and samples set off by different drumheads. During Crüe's Better Live than Dead tour for their *Red, White & Crüe* compilation, Lee had three complete drum sets: one onstage and two suspended twenty-five feet in the air, which he would fly between during his solo. The kit on stage right was probably metal's heaviest ever: a fifty-five-gallon oil drum and two beer kegs.

6. Joey Jordison (Slipknot)

The jazz-trained Jordison has used several rotating and tilting rigs himself, going Lee one better by having his drum kit spin horizontally like a turntable before tilting forward ninety degrees and spinning like a wheel of fortune—until the lights would go out, leaving the drum kit lit with a huge pentagram.

Metal Up Your Glasnost: The First 6 Western Heavy Metal Bands to Play Rock Festivals in Russia

The former Soviet Union got its first government-sanctioned taste of rock 'n' roll thanks to convicted drug smuggler Doc McGhee. Part of his sentence mandated he set up a charitable organization; that organization, the Make a Difference Foundation, sponsored the Moscow Music Peace Festival at Lenin Stadium in Moscow in 1989.

1. Skid Row
2. Cinderella
3. Bon Jovi
4. Mötley Crüe
5. Ozzy Osbourne
6. The Scorpions

The Russian metal band Gorky Park also played on the bill.

12 Heavy Metal Concept Albums, and Their Concepts

1. *A Black Moon Broods over Lemuria* (Bal-Sagoth)
Discovery of alien essence leads to worldwide death and destruction.

2. *Framing Armageddon (Something Wicked Part 1)* (Iced Earth)
The creation, the Apocalypse, and everything in between.

3. *Imaginos* (Blue Öyster Cult)
How Satan caused World War II.

4. *Maggots* (Plasmatics)
Man-eating maggots take a bite out of the Big Apple.

5. *Seventh Son of a Seventh Son* (Iron Maiden)
Bruce Dickinson wonders, "Where did we come from? Where are we going? And what does it all mean?"

6. *Still Life* (Opeth)
Lovesick loser comes for his true love, only to be hanged in the process. But at least they're together in death.

7. *Music from the Elder* (Kiss)

A hero-in-training sings about how tough it is to learn to save the world.

8. *A-Lex* (Sepultura)

A Clockwork Orange set to metal.

9. *The Crimson Idol* (W.A.S.P.)

Teenage loser–turned–rock star commits suicide when his parents *still* don't respect him.

10. *Leviathan* (Mastodon)

Moby-Dick gets the metal treatment.

11. *Streets: A Rock Opera* (Savatage)

The ups and downs of becoming a rock star, with an emphasis on the downs.

12. *Nostradamus* (Judas Priest)

The world mocks the French prophet's abilities until it's just . . . too . . . late.

Dave Thompson's 9 Subversive Metal Influences

1. The Kinks

By simply sticking knitting needles into an amplifier to try and make it sound dirtier, brothers Ray and Dave Davies were there at the birth of the beast. But add the primal crunch of "You Really Got Me" and "All Day and All of the Night," and they were midwives as well.

2. Bo Diddley

In the beginning, there was the Riff—and Bo built it. His own records are, to be truthful, no great shakes, but check out the Yardbirds' "I'm a Man" or Juicy Lucy's "Who Do Ya Love," and then come back.

3. Blue Cheer

Locked out of the house by Ma, the boys retired to the garage and jammed "Summertime Blues" until it slobbered on the floor. The blues never looked the same again.

4. Black Widow

You see, it isn't all skull-crushing riffs and trouser-taut vocals. Subject matter plays a

part as well, and if you think Sabbath are . . . ooh, scary and satanic . . . they're like a box of chocolates compared to the Widow.

5. Link Wray
Pete Townshend once described Wray's "The Rumble" as the most important guitar sound he ever heard. It probably was, as well.

6. The Yardbirds
A shoo-in, of course, because they gave us Eric Clapton, Jeff Beck, and Jimmy Page. But that's not why they're here. They're here because they also gave us "I'm a Man," "Happenings Ten Years Time Ago," and the prototype "Dazed and Confused." Much better.

7. The Stooges
The only band that made Blue Cheer sound slick, the Stooges perfected the clattering teen anthem, as nailed to a flat piece of wood. Add Ron Asheton's razor-perfect riffery and the first two Stooges albums crushed skulls for fun.

8. The Jeff Beck Group
Ex-Yardbirds, of course, but proto-Zeppelin; play Beck's *Truth* before *Led Zeppelin I* and you'll think your CD is stuck on repeat. Except the Beck album is better.

9. The Shadows
A rinky-dink English guitar band, right? All natty suits and shiny licks, right? Well, ask anybody who picked up an axe in the UK between 1959 and 1964 and they'll tell you. Page, Iommi, Beck, Blackmore, the lot. Everything they knew, they learned from the Shads.

British expat writer Dave Thompson has penned over 100 books. Seriously. He's the author of the highly acclaimed I Hate New Music: The Classic Rock Manifesto, *as well as books on Cream, Judas Priest, Jeff Beck, Deep Purple, David Bowie, Red Hot Chili Peppers, etc., etc., etc., and has contributed to* Rolling Stone, Alternative Press, MOJO, AllMusic Guide, *and* Melody Maker, *which gives him full license to expound on all things rock. Thompson resides in the little-known rock capital of Newark, Delaware.*

Dave Depraved of Blood Farmers' 6 Songs That Were Metal Before You Were Metal

1. "Breach of Lease"—Bloodrock

Bloodrock was a Texas band best known for "D.O.A.," a scary first-person account of a plane crash survivor's operating-table death throes. The organ-heavy dirge charted at number thirty-six after its initial release and later became an FM radio Halloween staple. Bloodrock followed up that blood-soaked bummer with "Breach of Lease," which amplifies the carnage from a mere airline disaster to the destruction of the entire planet. Front man Jim Rutledge delivers the dire folly-of-mankind lyrics over a creepy keyboard part that predictably swells to an apocalyptic Sabbath riff. Heavy, man. Other noteworthy Bloodrock nuggets include the psychedelic stomper "Melvin Laid an Egg," the Vietnam groove of "Kool-Aid Kids," and the redneck scare-tactics of "Whiskey Vengeance."

2. "Rumblin' Man"—Cactus

When their plan to join forces with Jeff Beck and Rod Stewart fell through, Tim Bogert and Carmine Appice of Vanilla Fudge formed this short-lived, would-be supergroup in an attempt to create America's answer to Led Zep. Completing the bombastic unit were two pedal-to-the-metal players from the Motor City: guitarist Jim McCarty of the Detroit Wheels and hard-living singer Rusty Day, who was later murdered along with his eleven-year-old son over a bad drug deal. Cactus forged some certified metal classics, including a methedrine-injected rendition of Mose Allison's "Parchman Farm" and a bone-crunching revamp of Howlin' Wolf's "Evil." But nowhere is the metallic excess of Cactus more glorious than in their insanely heavy interpretation of Link Wray's "Rumble," a sonic avalanche so brutal on the ears that no record company would release it for more than twenty-five years.

3. "Mesmerization Eclipse"—Captain Beyond

A knockout lead guitar line drives this track from the underappreciated Captain Beyond, which featured former members of Deep Purple and Iron Butterfly. The band had an original sound, with elements of Southern rock and heavy psyche-delia, but unjustly fell by the wayside after recording a couple of excellent LPs for Capricorn Records. A decade later, punk rock madman Tesco Vee tipped his codpiece to Captain B in the debauched Meatmen anthem "Pillar of Sodom." "Drugged-out visions of the dead in crypts / That dust be bringin' on a Mesmerization Eclipse!"

4. "Suicide"—Dust

Years before he became Marky Ramone, the young Marc Bell played drums in this New York power trio with guitarist/singer Richie Wise (later to produce the early

Kiss albums) and bassist Kenny Aaronson. Dust's two albums for Buddha Records offer energetic, pre-metal hard rock with a few nicely done Beatle ballads to break up the pace; they also boasted some of the era's coolest cover art. Standout tracks include the timeless metal imperative "Love Me Hard," "From a Dry Camel" (Dust's "Dazed and Confused," posing the philosophical question, "One hump, or two?"), and the karmic odyssey "Learning to Die." "Suicide" is a super-heavy '70s death-trip with a berserk bass solo and irresistible self-destructo lyrics: "Electrocution, I thought would make me a star / I stood in the rain, with my electric guitar!" The song's narrator then proceeds to stab himself through the heart and blow his own head off with a shotgun, just to eliminate any margin for error. Don't try this at home, says Richie today, reminding listeners that all three Dust dudes are still alive.

5. "The Master Heartache"—Sir Lord Baltimore

As a teenager, future Angry Samoans leader "Metal" Mike Saunders earned his nickname by using the term "heavy metal" for the very first time in a *Creem* magazine review of this New York group's debut album. Sir Lord Baltimore brought a streetwise, adrenalized attack to the template laid down by Cream and Hendrix, producing what many consider to be a forerunner of both punk and metal. "Master Heartache" shows SLB at their most inspired, blasting their way through a series of frantic, stop-and-start riffs barely held together by the overdrive antics of Gibson SG slinger Louis Dambra. Drummer/vocalist John Garner deserves special recognition for virtually inventing metal histrionics with his opening war cry of "Womaaaaaaan!"

6. "Potato Strut"—Swampgas

You may say I've lost all credibility here, and you're probably right. But listen and see if this unfortunately titled song doesn't compel the head to bang at the nodding pace usually associated with prescription drug abuse. Between singer Kim Ornitz growling incomprehensible metaphors for various sex acts, guitarist Baird Hersey peeling off mean Skynyrd-isms, and the whole band clamping down tight on a dirty backing riff, you've got the terminally obscure '70s metal tune that I defy anyone to cover.

Dave Szulkin (alias Dave Depraved) is the founder and guitarist of the doom metal band Blood Farmers (1989–1996), who gained a cult following for their self-titled debut on Germany's Hellhound Records. He is also the author of the acclaimed book Wes Craven's Last House on the Left: The Making of a Cult Classic, *and a producer of horror DVDs with Grindhouse Releasing. Tokyo-based Leafhound Records reissued the Blood Farmers' underground demo* Permanent Brain Damage, *which led to a reunion performance at Baltimore's Doom or Be Doomed festival and a Japanese tour in 2008. Szulkin lives in Los Angeles with his girlfriend, writer Virginia Pelley.*

15 METAL BANDS WHO USED TO PLAY IT PUNK

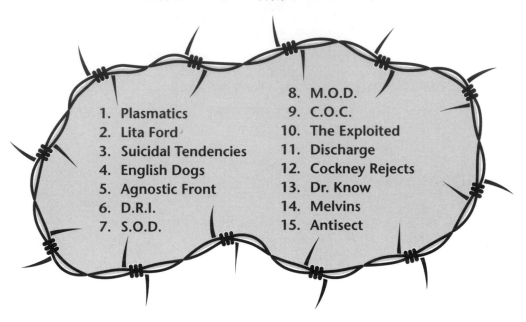

1. Plasmatics
2. Lita Ford
3. Suicidal Tendencies
4. English Dogs
5. Agnostic Front
6. D.R.I.
7. S.O.D.
8. M.O.D.
9. C.O.C.
10. The Exploited
11. Discharge
12. Cockney Rejects
13. Dr. Know
14. Melvins
15. Antisect

It's Fuckin' Metal, Dude!: 108 Genres and Subgenres, A to Z

1. Alternative metal
2. American power metal
3. Atmospheric sludge metal
4. Avant-garde metal
5. Beauty and the Beast
6. Bizarre metal
7. Black ambient (or ambient black metal)
8. Black doom
9. Black metal
10. Blackened death metal
11. Brutal death metal
12. Brutal death/grind
13. Brutal goregrind
14. Celtic metal
15. Chaotic death metal
16. Chaotic deathcore
17. Christian metal
18. Crustcore
19. Cyber goregrind
20. Cybergrind
21. Death doom
22. Death metal
23. Deathcore
24. Deathgrind
25. Doom metal
26. Drone doom
27. Electro pornogrind
28. Epic doom
29. Ethnic metal
30. European power metal
31. Experimental grind

32. Extreme industrial metal
33. Extreme metal
34. False metal
35. Folk metal
36. Funeral doom
37. Funk metal
38. Funkcore
39. Glam metal
40. Gore
41. Goregrind
42. Gothic black metal
43. Gothic metal
44. Grindcore
45. Grind 'n' roll
46. Groove metal
47. Groovy
48. Groovy grindcore
49. Hair metal
50. Hardcore metal
51. Heavy metal
52. Hero metal
53. Horror grind
54. Industrial metal
55. Manga pornogrind
56. Mathcore
57. Melodic black metal
58. Melodic death metal
59. Melodic heavy metal
60. Melodic power metal
61. Metalcore
62. Mincecore
63. Mittelalter rock
64. Modern Melodic death metal
65. Neo-classical metal
66. New Wave of British Heavy Metal
67. Noise
68. Noise/grind
69. Noisecore
70. Nü metal
71. Old school death metal
72. Oriental metal
73. Pagan metal
74. Ping-Pong gore grind zoo
75. Porncore
76. Pornogoregrind
77. Pornogrind
78. Post-metal
79. Power metal
80. Powerviolence
81. Progressive metal
82. Punk-funk
83. Rap metal
84. Sludge doom
85. Sludge metal
86. Speed metal
87. Stoner doom
88. Stoner metal
89. Stoner sludge metal
90. Symphonic black metal
91. Symphonic gothic metal
92. Symphonic metal
93. Symphonic power metal
94. Technical brutal death metal
95. Technical death metal
96. Technical/progressive death metal
97. Terror gore
98. Thrash metal
99. Thrash/death
100. Thrashcore
101. Tooth metal
102. Traditional doom
103. Traditional/Southern sludge metal
104. Unblack metal
105. Vampiric metal
106. Viking black metal
107. Viking metal
108. Wastecore

My Suite Satan: 5 Heavy Metal Bands Who Have Performed Live with a Symphony Orchestra

1. Deep Purple

The band played Jon Lord's *Concerto for Group and Orchestra*, originally a solo piece, with the Royal Philharmonic Orchestra in 1969 and the Los Angeles Philharmonic in 1970. That same year found the band playing another classical piece by Lord, *Gemini Suite*, with the Orchestra of the Light Music Society. *Concerto for Group and Orchestra* was replicated thirty years later with the London Symphony Orchestra, and still later with the George Enescu Philharmonic Orchestra and the New Japan Philharmonic Orchestra.

2. Metallica

The band killed 'em all with the CD *S&M Live with the San Francisco Orchestra*, conducted by Michael Kamen.

3. Kiss

Kiss Symphony: Alive VI caught the band with the Melbourne Symphony Orchestra. David Campbell conducted and did the arrangements.

4. Scorpions

Scorpions recorded *Moment of Glory* with the Berlin Philharmonic Orchestra; the work was conducted and arranged by Christian Kolonovits, who passed the baton to Scott Lawton on some dates of the ensemble's seven-city tour.

5. Queensrÿche

In 2008 the band played a set of their hits on a short tour with the Empire Orchestra.

21 All-Chick Metal Cover Bands

1. Slaywhore (Slayer)
2. Batholord (Bathory)
3. Kisses (Kiss)
4. Black Diamond (Kiss)
5. ThundHerStruck (AC/DC)
6. Whole Lotta Rosies (AC/DC)
7. Girls Girls Girls (Mötley Crüe)

8. Harptallica (Metallica)
9. Pinktallica (Metallica)
10. Hell's Belles (AC/DC)
11. The Iron Maidens (Iron Maiden)
12. Judith Priest (Judas Priest)
13. Malice Cooper (Alice Cooper)
14. Lez Zeppelin (Led Zeppelin)
15. Moby Chick (Led Zeppelin)
16. Zepparella (Led Zeppelin)
17. Turbonegra (Turbonegro)
18. Mistress of Reality (Black Sabbath)
19. The Little Dolls (Ozzy Osbourne)
20. Queen Diamond (King Diamond)
21. SheRuption (Van Halen)

Steph Paynes of Lez Zeppelin's 12 Things You Should Know if You Want to Play Guitar Like Jimmy Page

1. It's impossible to reach above the twelfth fret with the guitar hanging below your crotch. You'll have to bend over for most of the show.
2. Deciphering the guitar solo in "Heartbreaker" is virtually impossible, so you'll have to make something up that sounds just as cool and spontaneous. Also virtually impossible.
3. To play "Dazed and Confused" effectively with a violin bow, you'd be wise to first master the Mendelssohn Violin Concerto in E minor. Then, make sure you rosin the bow to proper stickiness, turn up the volume to shattering levels of sonic beauty, and make sure to properly set the slap-back on your Echoplex, else you shall not reverberate at all.
4. Sleeping with ten groupies and drinking an entire bottle of Jack Daniel's after each show will probably make you a little sloppy every once in a while. But it's definitely worth it.
5. You'll never sound like Jimmy unless you study and assimilate a wide variety of genres into your playing style, including: Celtic folk, like Burt Jansch; early rock 'n' roll à la Scotty Moore, Sonny Burgess, or Carl Perkins; country twang, like Albert Lee or Steve Cropper; seminal old blues, like Robert Johnson and Elmore James; some cool old jazz like Wes Montgomery; the '60s-influenced California sound of Joni Mitchell; and finally, some of the psychedelic folk/rock stylings of bands like the

Creation, the Pretty Things, Roy Harper, and Procol Harem. Then you'll have to practice for ten hours a day for at least five years. Ideally, if you could schedule an all-night jam session every week with Jeff Beck, that would be good too.

6. Often the Led Zeppelin tunes that sound most complex are the easiest to play. It's the early blues stuff that will reveal you for the impersonator you truly are!

7. Take the easy way out. When possible, play the solo in the same position and use the most obvious chord/scale formations. As Jimmy said, "Why struggle?"

8. You'd be wise to begin with .008 gauge strings, since you'll have to bend every other note past the bleeding point of your soon-to-be-ironclad calluses.

9. If you can't master Jimmy's quivering vibrato, try drinking until you get the DTs. That's been known to help.

10. There's no consistent count between the riffs in "Black Dog," so stop trying to figure it out and learn to play by feel.

11. Emotion over technique any and every day. (But first, you will need to be a virtuoso).

12. Finally, "Do as thou wilt," and you may stand half a chance.

Steph Paynes is the founder and guitarist of Lez Zeppelin, an all-girl band based in New York City that plays the music of Led Zeppelin. Since its formation in 2004, the band has gained critical acclaim around the world not only for their powerful and exuberant performances, but for serving as a "she-incarnation" of one of the world's most beloved bands. Paynes has also been known to write a novel or two and has had a fairly extensive career as a music journalist. Her writing has appeared in Rolling Stone, New Musical Express, Musician, Playboy, *and* Guitar Player, *among many other publications.*

The Song Retains the Name: 15 Unusual Metal Cover Bands

1. Cannabis Corpse
They play pot-themed parodies of Cannibal Corpse songs.

2. Black Sweden
The ultimate meeting of good and evil, performing black metal versions of ABBA tunes.

3. Hayseed Dixie
AC/DC performed bluegrass style.

4. Van Hayride
Van Halen performed bluegrass style.

5. The Misfats
Very fat guys cover Misfits songs with titles like "Mommy, Can I Go Out and Grill Tonight?" and "I Turned into a Lardass."

6. Cookie Mongoloid
The musical vehicle of a California comedy troupe, Cookie Mongoloid plays speed metal covers of *Sesame Street* songs. The death-growling lead singer wears a Cookie Monster mask.

7. Dread Zeppelin
A reggae Led Zeppelin cover band fronted by a black Elvis impersonator.

8. Evil Trio
If you've ever wanted to hear jazz versions of Iron Maiden songs in Swedish, this band is for you.

9. Tunna Liza
Swedish acoustic versions of Thin Lizzy songs.

10. Game Over
Swedish heavy metal video game theme-song covers!

11. Metalshop
This cover band can play as six different bands in one night.

12. MiniKiss
A Kiss cover band made up of three dwarves and a midget.

13. Tiny Kiss
Another little-person Kiss cover band.

14. Rondellus

Rondellus plays Black Sabbath songs on original medieval instruments, with vocals in Latin.

15. Tragedy

A heavy metal Bee Gees cover band.

Ice-T of Body Count's 11 Favorite Heavy Metal Bands

1. Cannibal Corpse
2. Black Sabbath
3. Pantera
4. Slayer
5. Motörhead
6. Anthrax
7. Megadeth
8. Sepultura
9. AC/DC
10. Blue Öyster Cult
11. Deep Purple

Ice-T is an original gangster who has conquered rap and metal worlds by fronting the controversial metal outfit Body Count. He has appeared in movies including New Jack City *and* Johnny Mnemonic *and has played Detective Odafin "Fin" Tutuola on* Law & Order: Special Victims Unit *since 2000.*

Joel McIver of *Record Collector* Magazine's List of 10 Most Valuable Heavy Metal Vinyls

1. "Twilight Zone" / "Wrathchild"—Iron Maiden

7-inch single with picture sleeve, brown vinyl mispressing, EMI 5145, 1981; £650

2. "Children of the Grave"—Black Sabbath b/w "Roadhouse Blues"—Status Quo

7-inch single, 100 promo copies only, Phonogram DJ 005, 1972; £400

3. *Black Metal*—Venom

LP, green marbled vinyl, Neat NEAT 1005, 1982; £350

4. The Def Leppard EP: "Ride into the Sun" / "Getcha Rocks Off" / "The Overture"—Def Leppard

7-inch, red label, picture sleeve with lyric insert, 150 only, Bludgeon Riffola SRT/CUS/232, 1979; £300

5. "Holy Smoke" / "All in Your Mind" / "Kill Me Ce Soir"—Iron Maiden
12-inch, gold vinyl test pressing, promo only, EMI 12EMP 158, 1990; £250

6. "Too Late for Love" / "Foolin' "—Def Leppard
7-inch single, picture sleeve, DJ-only promo with rear band photo in football kit, Phonogram VERDJ 8, 1983; £150

7. *Best of the Beast*—Iron Maiden
CD, Steve Harris interview disc, commercial CD, video, in 40cm x 30cm, flip-up 3-D presentation box with 60-page book, two photographs, biography, promo only, EMI BEST 001, 1996; £150

8. *The Soundhouse Tapes*—Iron Maiden
EP, p/s; counterfeits have slightly glossier sleeves, Rock Hard ROK 1, 1979; £125

9. *The Metallican*—Metallica
CD, gold disc in metal paint can with video & T-shirt; 35,000 only, Vertigo MECAN 1/510-022-0, 1991; £100

10. "Evil Woman" / "Wicked World"—Black Sabbath
7-inch single, Fontana TF 1067, 1970; £100

Compiled by Joel McIver with thanks to Record Collector *magazine's Rare Record Price Guide. Joel is a contributor to many rock and metal magazines and is the author of twelve books, including the best-selling* Justice for All: The Truth About Metallica *(Omnibus Press, 2004).*

9 Non-Metal Bands That Do a Song Called "Heavy Metal"
1. Clap Your Hands Say Yeah
2. Guy Clark
3. Les Cowboys Fringants
4. The City of Prague Philharmonic
5. Stockholm Chamber Brass
6. Miles Davis
7. The Beatings
8. Steven Halpern
9. Young Jeezy and Fabolous

False Metal: 6 Mainstream Artists Who Have Covered Metal Songs

1. Celine Dion
The Canadian song stylist sings a notoriously bad version of "Back in Black."

2. Dolly Parton
Dolly is one of several artists to record "Stairway to Heaven."

3. Shakira
Shakira performed "Back in Black" and "Dude Looks Like a Lady" during her Tour of the Mongoose.

4. Lesley Gore
The '60s pop legend covers "Dirty Deeds Done Dirt Cheap" by AC/DC on the CD *When Pigs Fly: Songs You Never Thought You'd Hear.*

5. Mariah Carey
Sang Def Leppard's "Bringin' on the Heartbreak" on her CD *Rainbows.*

6. Pat Boone
Pat did an entire album of metal covers called *In a Metal Mood: No More Mr. Nice Guy* that includes
1. "You've Got Another Thing Comin'"—Judas Priest
2. "Smoke on the Water"—Deep Purple
3. "It's a Long Way to the Top (If You Wanna Rock 'N' Roll)"—AC/DC
4. "Panama"—Van Halen
5. "No More Mr. Nice Guy"—Alice Cooper
6. "Love Hurts"—Nazareth (originally by the Everly Brothers)
7. "Enter Sandman"—Metallica
8. "Holy Diver"—Dio
9. "Paradise City"—Guns N' Roses
10. "The Wind Cries Mary"—The Jimi Hendrix Experience
11. "Crazy Train"—Ozzy Osbourne
12. "Stairway to Heaven"—Led Zeppelin

Thick as a Brick: 21 Years of Metal Grammy Winners

1988
Best Hard Rock/Metal Performance, Vocal or Instrumental
Jethro Tull
Crest of a Knave

1989
Best Metal Performance
Metallica
"One"

1990
Best Metal Performance
Metallica
"Stone Cold Crazy"

1991
Best Metal Performance
Metallica
Metallica

1992
Best Metal Performance with Vocal
Nine Inch Nails
"Wish"

1993
Best Metal Performance with Vocal
Ozzy Osbourne
"I Don't Want to Change the World"

1994
Best Metal Performance with Vocal
Soundgarden
"Spoonman"

1995
Best Metal Performance
Nine Inch Nails
"Happiness in Slavery"

1996
Best Metal Performance
Rage Against the Machine
"Tire Me"

1997
Best Metal Performance
Tool
"Aenema"

1998
Best Metal Performance
Metallica
"Better Than You"

1999
Best Metal Performance
Black Sabbath
"Iron Man"

2000
Best Metal Performance
Deftones
"Elite"

2001
Best Metal Performance
Tool
"Schism"

2002
Best Metal Performance
Korn
"Here to Stay"

2003
Best Metal Performance
Metallica
"St. Anger"

2004
Best Metal Performance
Motörhead
"Whiplash"

2005
Best Metal Performance
Slipknot
"Before I Forget"

2006
Best Metal Performance
Slayer
"Eyes of the Insane"

2007
Best Metal Performance
Slayer
"Final Six"

2008
Best Metal Performance
Metallica
"My Apocalypse"

100 (Mainly) Instrumental Heavy Metal Acts

1. Blotted Science
2. Canvas Solaris
3. Ghost Snorter
4. Raven Blayde
5. Carlos Lichman
6. Billy Crystal Meth
7. Erik Norlander
8. Craig Goldbaum
9. Curt Shaw
10. A.M.P.
11. Bongripper
12. Fretboard
13. Nacho Mur
14. Ageless Kingdoms
15. Mountains Became Machines
16. Amphigory
17. The Great Kat
18. Paranormal Activity
19. Chronic Infestation
20. Matthew Mills
21. Laurent Fleury
22. Chris Brooks
23. Iron Dragon
24. Hanswer
25. George Bellas
26. Fact & Fiction
27. Pelican
28. Joshua Van Der Stam's Anaconda
29. Spiritus Mundi
30. Mythic Force
31. Sammach

32. Ribcage Rupture
33. Mills of God
34. Qwestion
35. Alison Hell
36. Psychotic Existence
37. Monsanto
38. Kong
39. Adrian Raso
40. John Petrucci
41. Jagged Eye
42. Fatal Strike
43. Sean Malone
44. Electro Quarterstaff
45. Chejron
46. Aethenor
47. Tony Hernando
48. Andy James
49. Thomas Bressel
50. Shane Gibson
51. Up from the Grave
52. Toby Knapp
53. Asteroidea
54. Sleep Terror
55. Beast in the Field
56. The Ludovico Technique
57. Misogyny
58. Tarantula Hawk
59. Stefan Hancu
60. Abolishment of Hate
61. Reckoning Storm
62. Neutron Crush
63. Super String Theory
64. Parallaxe
65. Jitterbug
66. Satanic Sega Genesis
67. Omega Massif
68. Mothertrucker
69. The Fucking Champs
70. Back Pain
71. Sam Kazerooni
72. Rigid Horns
73. Metatronik
74. Pseudovoid
75. Poles Apart
76. Dreams of Dying Stars
77. Electrocution 250
78. Michael Romeo
79. Dysrhythmia
80. Sonic Hispeed Omega
81. Devil in the Kitchen
82. Nofertum
83. Randy Blair
84. Horsefang
85. Derek Sherinian
86. Jeremy Krull
87. Hermetic Brotherhood
88. Dave Byron
89. Malfunction
90. Katrina Johansson
91. Loincloth
92. La Era de Ophiucus
93. Leviathan
94. John Ferns
95. Like Drone Razors Through Flesh Sphere
96. KF Project
97. Marty Friedman
98. Gynecrology
99. Davide Marrari
100. Metatronik

Listen to the Flower People: 13 Weird-Ass Heavy Metal Instruments

Celtic and folk metal have both introduced scores of exotic instruments into the genre. Here are some.

1. Tin whistle
Cruachan uses this traditional six-holed woodwind instrument, with a range of a seventh.

2. Bodhran
An open-ended Irish frame drum whose pitch is determined by pressing against the goatskin head with your hand from the inside.

3. Bombard
A double-reed instrument also called a talabard, used by Aes Dana.

4. Irish bouzouki
Small eight-stringed instrument like a mandolin.

5. Bagpipes
A reed instrument given a constant stream of air through a bag the piper blows into and squeezes. Used by In Extremo.

6. Hurdy-gurdy
A stringed instrument you play with a crank. Metallica used one on "Low Man's Lyric."

7. Shawm
The woodwind instrument that gave us the oboe. Also used by In Extremo.

8. Barrel organ
A pipe organ that plays music written onto wooden cylinders that are moved with a crank.

9. Glockenspiel
You can hear SuidAkrA play this German xylophone.

10. Lute

Eluveitie incorporate this mandolin-type instrument from Europe that can have from fifteen to twenty-eight strings.

11. Uilleann pipes

Irish bagpipes.

12. Accordion

The thing Weird Al Yankovic plays. The Celtic metal band Turisas plays one too.

13. Kantele

A zitherlike Finnish instrument with up to forty strings. Used by Korpiklaani.

Crazy Train: 10 Unusual Metal Bands

1. Stovokor

Making their earthly base in Portland, Oregon, Stovokor boldly goes where no metal band has gone before by performing their "Metal of Honor" in Klingon. Stovokor crew members are pInluH HoD on "vocals and orders"; guitarists Khr'ell and Che'ron mucHwl; Khraa'nik on bass; and Qui PeJ playing "war drums."

2. Beatallica

Jaymz OH!NOOO! Lennfield, Kliff McBurtney, Grg Hammetson, and Ringo Larz play Beatles parodies in the musical style of Metallica. The band has performed with Motörhead, Sepultura, Kreator, and Sammy Hagar, and their first CD, *Sgt. Hetfield's Motorbreath Pub Band*, is a ticket to ride the lightning with songs including "And Justice for All My Loving," "A Garage Dayz Nite," and "Leper Madonna." Lars Ulrich once loaned the band his lawyer when Sony/ATV, owners of rights to lots of Beatles songs, hit the band with a cease-and-desist order.

3. Brother Cesare Bonizzi

Sixty-two-year-old Brother Cesare is an Italian Franciscan monk who fronts the metal band Fratello Metallo ("Brother Metal," which is also his nickname). His conversion to metal came after seeing a performance by Metallica.

4. Caninus

Twin vocalists for this Brooklyn-based grindcore band really have the death growl down—because they're pit bulls named Basil and Budgie.

5. Hatebeak

Lead vocals for Hatebeak are provided by Waldo, a fifteen-year-old parrot.

6. Hatred

This prepubescent four-member Scottish metal band's search for a new bassist was chronicled in the television special *Heavy Metal Jr.* Their very own Spinal Tap moment comes when a band member's mother has matching denim jackets made up for them, with the band name misspelled "Hatrid."

7. Van Canto

This German six-piece does it a cappella, their only instrumentalist being drummer Bastian Emig. Their melodic metal, with its elements of choral and vocalese set against driving drum beats, soars on original compositions as well as covers of songs by Deep Purple, Iron Maiden, Nightwish, and Manowar.

8. 12 Ton Method

This British metal band bases its approach to music on the "twelve-tone method" (also called dodecaphony or serialism) pioneered by composer Arnold Schoenberg in 1921. Its basis is that all twelve notes of a chromatic scale are played in equal relation to one another, so that a composition is not in any particular key. This musical discipline was later taken up by composers including Igor Stravinsky and Pierre Boulez (an influence upon and collaborator with Frank Zappa).

9. Anakron

Hungarian performer Györffy András is the sole member of this folk metal band, whose recorded music is instrumental but comes with a set of lyrics (presumably) to be read while the music plays. Most of his recorded output remains unreleased.

10. Bang Camaro

This metal act from Boston uses between ten and twenty lead singers during their live gigs.

Pete Fry of Rockarma and FarCry's 6 Songs That Almost Made Me Quit Playing Guitar

All of these songs were extremely frustrating to me as a young player, but I finally came to grips with the fact that not everyone will be a techno-wizard. But that still doesn't mean you have to end up asking, "You want fries with that?"

1. "The Explorer"—Shotgun Messiah

Oh my God, where the hell did this Harry Cody guy come from? Maybe I should "explore" a different instrument. He's a phenomenal (and underrated) player, but I'm not sure what he's doing now.

2. "Far Beyond the Sun"—Yngwie J. Malmsteen's Rising Force

I bought this on vinyl back when you could only get it as a Japanese import. It was recommended to me by a teacher at my high school who also owned a record store. "You play guitar. You definitely have to get this!" he said. I was blown away. Nobody was playing like this back then.

3. "Mr. Scary"—Dokken

George Lynch was one of my earliest metal influences after seeing them open for Dio on Dokken's tour supporting *Tooth and Nail*. The tone, the attack, and the speed were unbelievable on this track, and it seemed like he got exponentially better on every album. This still holds up today and people are still emulating his style—including Jon Levin, Dokken's current guitarist.

4. "Cemetary Gates"—Pantera

I was never much of a fan of their heavier stuff, but Dimebag could put some serious hooks together. On top of that, his solos were fast as hell and tasteful, somewhat unusual for Pantera's style of music. And his tone was completely his own.

5. "Play with Me"—Extreme

After dismissing the first single I heard ("Kid Ego") as not all that, I picked up the album anyway. After hearing that this Nuno Bettencourt guy had some chops, I was completely baffled by his ability to blend amazingly fast scalar runs with odd melodies in a seemingly effortless manner. For a long time Nuno was hands-down my favorite player. There's nothing he can't play.

6. "Scarified"—Racer X

After hearing the studio version of this, I picked up Racer X's *Live: Extreme Volume* and was amazed to hear them do this incredibly intricate and blindingly fast instrumental stuff, packed full of guitar harmonies and difficult breaks, in a live setting. It's still amazing when I listen to it now.

Pete Fry has been playing guitar for over twenty-five years and is currently the lead guitarist for Kivel Records recording artists Rockarma and FarCry.

12 GIBSON FLYING V GUITARISTS

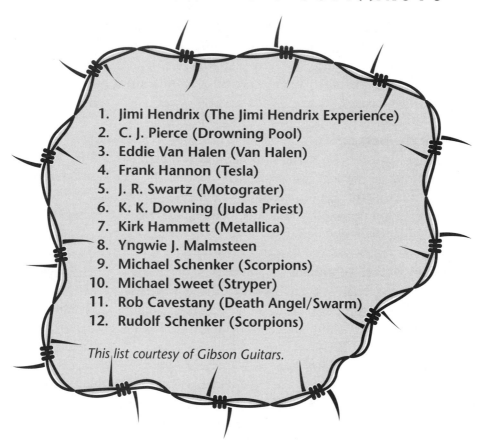

1. Jimi Hendrix (The Jimi Hendrix Experience)
2. C. J. Pierce (Drowning Pool)
3. Eddie Van Halen (Van Halen)
4. Frank Hannon (Tesla)
5. J. R. Swartz (Motograter)
6. K. K. Downing (Judas Priest)
7. Kirk Hammett (Metallica)
8. Yngwie J. Malmsteen
9. Michael Schenker (Scorpions)
10. Michael Sweet (Stryper)
11. Rob Cavestany (Death Angel/Swarm)
12. Rudolf Schenker (Scorpions)

This list courtesy of Gibson Guitars.

10 Fun Facts About the Gibson EDS 1275 Double Neck Guitar

1. Jimmy Page did not invent the double neck guitar.

Page is the guitarist most synonymous with the double neck, but he didn't invent it. It was originally released in 1958, the same year Gibson released the Explorer and the Flying V.

2. It's two, two, two guitars in one! A twelve-string, and a six-string!

Yeah, but it wasn't always. There were two models of double neck: one with a twelve-string and six-string configuration, and another that was called the double mandolin, which had one neck with six strings and another, smaller-scale neck designed to sound like a mandolin.

3. You can't go into just any old guitar shop and buy one.

Gibson now only makes custom versions of the guitar.

4. Jimmy Page is not the only guitarist to play the EDS 1275 double neck.

Other guitarists who have strapped one on include Alex Lifeson of Rush, Don Felder of the Eagles, and Davey Johnstone.

5. You can only get the EDS 1275 in cherry (like Page's) or white.

It was previously also crafted in tobacco burst and black.

6. The EDS 1275 wasn't always a solid-body guitar.

When first introduced, the guitar was a hollowbody. The solid-body model was released in 1962.

7. Jimmy Page only played the EDS 1275 in the studio on one song.

That song was "Carouselambra" from *In Through the Out Door*.

8. The EDS 1275 was the first electric twelve-string guitar.

9. The EDS 1275 weighs thirteen pounds.

10. The Gibson double neck is the coolest guitar in the world!

As a matter of fact, it is, according to the editors of gigwise.com, who in 2008 chose the 30 Coolest Guitars in the World. Other metal axes appearing on their list are

Slash's B. C. Rich Mockingbird; Buckethead's Jackson Y2KV; Dave Mustaine's Dean VMNT; the Queensrÿche ESP guitar (based on the band's logo); Bumblefoot's Vigier "Bumblefoot" guitar—a black-and-yellow foot-shaped body with bee wings; John Paul Jones' triple neck arch-top mandolin by Manson, with two mandolin necks and a bass neck; and Michael Angelo Batio's Quad guitar.

This list written in collaboration with Gibson Guitars.

29 Metalheads with Signature Model Guitars

1. Malcolm Young (AC/DC)
Gretsch Guitars G6131MY Malcolm Young II signature electric guitar

2. Angus Young (AC/DC)
Gibson Angus Young signature SG

3. Buck Dharma (Blue Öyster Cult)
J. C. Harper Buck Dharma Signature model guitar

4. Dave Mustaine (Megadeth)
Dean Dave Mustaine Signature VMNT electric guitar

5. Marty Friedman (Megadeth)
Jackson KE1 Marty Friedman model

6. Kirk Hammett (Metallica)
ESP LTD KH-602 Kirk Hammett signature guitar

7. James Hetfield (Metallica)
ESP Truckster James Hetfield signature guitar

8. Michael Angelo Batio
Dean MAB 1 Armorflame

9. Dimebag Darrell (Damageplan)
Dean USA Razorback Tribute Dimebag Darrell signature guitar

10. Eddie Van Halen (Van Halen)
EVH Wolfgang guitar

11. Gary Holt (Exodus)
ESP Alex Laiho LTD-AL-600 signature guitar

12. Jay Jay French (Twisted Sister)
Epiphone Jay Jay French Twisted Pinkburst signature guitar

13. Jimmy Page (Led Zeppelin)
Gibson Custom Shop Jimmy Page signature Les Paul

14. Tony Iommi (Black Sabbath)
Epiphone Tony Iommi Signature G-400 electric guitar

15. Joe Satriani
Ibanez JS1200 Joe Satriani signature guitar

16. John 5 (Marilyn Manson)
Fender J5 Triple Tele Deluxe

17. Steve Vai
Ibanez Steve Vai Bad Horsie: JEM signature guitar

18. Yngwie J. Malmsteen
Fender Stratocaster Yngwie Malmsteen signature guitar

19. Kerry King (Slayer)
B.C. Rich KKV Kerry King signature guitar

20. Matt DeVries (Chimaira)
The LTD MFA-600 Matt DeVries electric guitar

21. Will Adler (Lamb of God)
ESP LTD WA600 Will Adler signature guitar

22. Michael Schenker (Michael Schenker Group)
The Dean Michael Schenker Standard guitar

23. Mick Mars (Mötley Crüe)

The Kramer Mirror Top Telecaster

24. Mick Thomson (Slipknot)

Ibanez MTM1 Mick Thomson signature guitar

25. Gene Simmons (Kiss)

The Gene Simmons Axe (shaped like a battle axe) from Kramer

26. Paul Stanley (Kiss)

The "Cracked Mirror" Iceman from Ibanez

27. Zakk Wylde (Black Label Society)

Zakk Wylde Signature Les Paul Custom

28. Phil Collen (Def Leppard)

Jackson USA PC 1 Phil Collen signature guitar

29. Slash (Guns N' Roses)

The Slash Custom Les Paul

Mike Edison's 5 Greatest Heavy Metal Gimmicks (and One Truly Pathetic Attempt)

1. Kiss

Fire-breathing, blood-spitting Demon trumps the Giant Kitty Kat every time. 'Nuff said.

2. AC/DC

Not just for the schoolboy uniform. Also the cannons, Hell's Bell, the inflatable Rosie, the Heatseeker Missile, and my favorite, Angus dollars.

3. Alice Cooper

Not horror rock, shock rock. Electric chairs, guillotines, Billion Dollar Babies.

4. Screaming Lord Sutch and Heavy Friends

Here's an idea: Hire half of Led Zeppelin to be your backup band. Unless they aren't available, in which case get Jeff Beck and whoever else is lurking around the pub, like Jimi Hendrix's bass player.

5. Black Sabbath

By no means the first horror-rock band, but by far the best. Ozzy's voice itself rates as a top gimmick in these parts. Special mention for Sab's giant Stonehenge used on the *Born Again* tour, which was too big to bring through the loading bays of about half the hockey rinks in America and gave way to a key Spinal Tap gag.

One Truly Pathetic Attempt

KISS unmasked

Your gimmick is, uh, no gimmick? Really, who gives a fuck?

Former High Times *publisher Mike Edison is the author of twenty-eight pornographic novels, and the memoir* I Have Fun Everywhere I Go: Savage Tales of Pot, Porn, Punk Rock, Pro Wrestling, Talking Apes, Evil Bosses, Dirty Blues, American Heroes, and the Most Notorious Magazines in the World. *He is also the putative editor of this book.*

2008 World Air Guitar Champion Hot Lixx Hulahan's 8 Tips for Successful Air Guitar

1. Unless you're trying to emulate Phil Collins or the bad Metallica years, you'll need long hair. If you try rocking out with short hair, you run the risk of looking like you're play air key-tar.
2. You've got a tongue: Use it. Better yet, abuse it.
3. You're not visually blocked by an actual guitar, so take advantage by over-expressing things with your hips, pelvis, crotch, and untethered wang.
4. Your outfit is crucial. Wear every ridiculously flamboyant piece of clothing you can dig up. Raid your mom's closet for scarves, fishnets, and something to stuff down your pants. If by some strange twist of fate you no longer live in your parents' basement and lack access to such fashions, G-E-T N-A-K-E-D. Rock out with your cock out!
5. Much like masturbation, air guitaring was born in the bedroom under threat of discovery, so just ditch the shame and you'll notice a marked improvement. This goes for air guitaring, too.

6. Think big. Make sure those people in the back can see your radness.
7. Remember that your target demographic—the people with whom you want to share nameless backstage sex—want you for your willingness to put yourself out there and not necessarily for your looks or talent. Cases in point: Keith Richards and Nickelback, respectively.
8. Lastly, go all out! You're playing air guitar—what else have you got to lose?

Hot Lixx Hulahan is the 2008 World Air Guitar Champion. For heavy metal street cred he offers his formative years spent growing up in the Bay Area during the apex of its thrash and speed metal era. He was the type to wear Gene Loves Jezebel shirts to Death Angel shows and do against-the-current somersaults in the pit.

11 Things That Have Happened Between the Release of Guns N' Roses' *The Spaghetti Incident?* and *Chinese Democracy*

1. Slash, Duff McKagan, Izzy Stradlin, and Matt Sorum release 22 full albums between them. Even Steven Adler releases an EP.
2. The Beatles issue three new singles.
3. Viagra is patented.
4. Grunge becomes the drug of choice for America's youth, replacing heavy metal.
5. Kurt Cobain commits suicide.
6. Heavy metal again becomes the drug of choice for America's youth, replacing grunge.
7. Apple introduces the MP3, giving sixteen-year-old kids a novel way to leak tracks from *Chinese Democracy*.
8. America elects its first black president.
9. The first module of the International Space Station makes 57,400 orbits around the earth.
10. Approximately 150,000 porn films are released.
11. Led Zeppelin reforms.

CHAPTER 6

⊕N ✝HE R⊕AD

The 7 Wonders of the Metal World

1. Birmingham, England

This industrial factory town is the most metal city on the planet. John Bonham and Robert Plant of Led Zeppelin hail from here, as do members of Judas Priest and Black Sabbath. It's also the site of the sheet metal factory where Tony Iommi lost the tips of two fingers in a machining accident; that accident caused him to detune his guitar so he could play with a minimum of pain, which gave Black Sabbath—and heavy metal itself—its signature sound. The town praises its own, too, having established a Walk of Fame, where both Ozzy Osbourne and Iommi are honored with brass star plaques.

2. Mr. S Leather
London

Run alternately out of a small storefront and the trunk of the owner's car, Mr. S Leather was the Soho leather fetish shop where Rob Halford bought his leather gear, giving Judas Priest and all who came after their hard-rocking look. The fact that that look had its roots in London's gay underground was lost on many until Halford came out of the closet. The store was eventually sold and relocated by its new owners to San Francisco.

3. Hyatt West Hollywood Hotel
Los Angeles, CA

Now known as the Andaz West Hollywood, the former Hyatt Hotel will always be known as the Riot House in honor of the spectacular displays of rock 'n' roll destruction and debauchery that took place within its halls in the '70s. The Riot House was home to bands like the Doors, the Who, and the Rolling Stones; the fun and games there usually hit their zenith when Led Zeppelin came to town; this is the place where Bonzo rode a motorcycle down the halls and took part in that time-honored rock-star tradition, throwing televisions out of the window. It's also the spot where Lemmy reportedly wrote the song "Motörhead."

4. Bandwagon Soundhouse
London

The Soundhouse gave heavy metal two of its most famous commodities: Iron Maiden and air guitar. DJ Neal Kay hit pay dirt when he took this part-time discotheque down the road to heavy metal history by having weekly hard-rock parties. As word spread, the club gained a reputation as the place to hear the best and newest rock bands, including Iron Maiden, who set up a residency there after Kay played one of their demos. The Soundhouse also gave birth to the art of air guitar when young headbangers, determined to get as far into Kay's playlist as possible, began making their own guitars out of cardboard to play along with the records.

5. 96 and 98 St. Marks Place
New York, NY

This building in New York City's East Village is featured on the front cover of Led Zep's album *Physical Graffiti*. At the time, *Physical Graffiti* was not only a highly anticipated and memorable evolution in Zep's sound, but thanks to the dozens of die-cut windows in its artwork, boasted one of the most expensive album covers of its day. The storefront of the building is now an antique clothing store, named Physical Graffiti.

6. Montreux Casino
Montreux, Switzerland

If Frank Zappa and the Mothers of Invention hadn't played here, and some stupid with a flare gun hadn't burned the place to the ground, and Glenn Hughes hadn't watched smoke billow across the river, metal might not have gained one of it most famous songs and most memorable, easy-to-play riffs: "Smoke on the Water."

7. Seventh Veil Strip Club
Los Angeles

On any given night in the '80s you could find members of the Sunset Strip's best (and worst) glam bands at the Seventh Veil, gettin' drunk and stuffin' the muffins of nubile young dancers with dollar bills (or something a little more substantial); the club was memorialized in Mötley Crüe's tune "Girls Girls Girls." A fire ravaged it in late 2008, and a nation of cock rockers mourned.

Ron "Bumblefoot" Thal's 10 Lamest Things Anyone Said to Me Right Before Playing a Show

1. "I can't fight my demons anymore. I'm quitting the tour and quitting playing music forever."

This was said by my drummer in 2002, on the third show of a European tour, with three more weeks left to play. The drummer of the opening act learned all our songs overnight and played the next show with us, while a friend finished his band's tour and flew down from Germany, learning our songs with headphones on the plane. We finished the tour without missing a show.

2. "I'm not making as much money from album sales as I'd like. I want your worldwide publishing income."

The head of a little French label I licensed one album to, picking a fight with me about wanting to take my publishing, literally as I was walking up the stairs onto the stage saying, "Can we please discuss this later? I have to play a show now."

3. *silence*

The in-house monitor engineer at a venue in France, who should have worked out technical issues with us *before* the show, rather than *during* the show.

4. "I'm sorry, the amp we have for you is broken, but maybe you can still get some little bit of sound out of it."

I heard this in 1997 in France, right before starting a guitar clinic with a room of a hundred people waiting.

5. "Dude, you can't wear that shirt onstage. It's yellow!"

A band member in 2006. Not really a lame thing to say, considering the shirt also had a big picture of me dressed up like a nerd pointing and saying, "Hello, my name is Ronald, and your name is douchebag!" No one had a problem with what was on the shirt, only the fact that the shirt was yellow.

6. "Wow, you must be stupid."

A bar owner said this to me in 1993, when I was playing a cover gig in a friend's band at a tiny local bar in Staten Island, New York. It was his response when I politely asked if he had masking tape—which he did. He couldn't believe I would come to his fine establishment without bringing my own masking tape, and went on and on about it as if I didn't have my guitar with me. I was the first band member there, so maybe one of the other guys had some? I didn't stick around to find out. When the guy called me stupid, I packed up my stuff and walked out. He said, "Where ya goin'?" I said, "Home," with a smile and left. In my absence, he told the next band member to arrive that I'd "never play this town again." He sure showed me.

7. "Fine, *you* can headline now!"

While playing a venue in NYC, we were one of the opening acts, scheduled to go on right before the headliner. The drummer of the headlining act wanted to go on earlier and complained to me that there were too many bands playing that night, and he was tired. I kindly suggested that he discuss it with the club owner, adding that I didn't have the authority to make those kinds of decisions, but I'd be willing to cut my set short, if that would help. He responded with the above remark and stormed off.

8. "Hurry up. Hurry up. Hurry up!"

The story continues.... The promoter was going to boot us off the bill so the headliner could go on earlier. They were undecided, told us not to set up our equipment, waited until five minutes before we were supposed to go on, and gave us the okay to play. With just five minutes to set everything up, they raised the curtains and kept saying into the monitors, "Hurry up. Hurry up," over and over, with the audience watching, until we started playing. My tech was still setting up my amp and I played without a guitar, just singing for the first the songs until the gear was ready.

9. "No."

We were opening for an '80s hair band at a local New York City club in 1993. There was a nice spread of food backstage, and the band let it be known that we couldn't have any, but my wife (my girlfriend at the time) could. She declined. We were told they'd brought their own power generator and that all the gear onstage, including our, had to be connected to it. We started playing our set, and thirty seconds into the first song, our power was shut off. They said there was a problem with the generator. We waited, the audience waited. Miraculously, the problem got fixed five minutes before they were scheduled to start playing. Being that we were onstage with guitars in hand, all set up, we asked if we could at least play one song for all the people who had come down to the show to see us (which was the majority of the audience, being as we were the support act with the local draw.) They said, "No." I won't say who the band was, only that I'll always remember them as a bunch of Dix.

10. "Wussup everyone? My name is Mya! It's wonderful to be here!"

I said this, in 2003, on a big stage at Six Flags Amusement Park in New Jersey. I was playing guitar in a friend's rock band, and we were supposed to open for Avril Lavigne, but at the last minute the headliner changed to R&B hip-hop artist Mya; we were totally mismatched. It was pretty cold on the night of the show, and they wouldn't let us have any of the dressing rooms, so we got changed in our cars, and waited in them with the heat on. The audience was chanting for Mya—the last thing they wanted was a bunch of white kids playing '80s-new-wave-inspired quirky rock. So I figured I'd nail the coffin shut and go all out. Showtime, I walked to the front of the stage wearing a silver tux and no pants, just silk boxers with hearts on them. I stepped up to the microphone and said, "Wussup everyone? My name is Mya! It's wonderful to be here!" Thousands of completely confused people fell into awkward silence. You could truly hear nothing but crickets. It was like that moment of pure peace, just before you drown. We played, as people chanted, "We want Mya!" and pelted us with pens, coins, and whatever else they could part with.

A recording artist and since the early '90s, Bumblefoot has released nine CDs and a live DVD; his latest solo discs are Abnormal *and the acoustic EP* Barefoot. *He's been a member of Guns N' Roses since 2006 and plays on the band's* Chinese Democracy *CD. He also writes music for TV shows, loves extreme hot sauce (boasting a tolerance of over 7 million Scoville units), takes oral hygiene and fire safety very seriously, and if you need someone to install drywall or do electrical work, he's your guy.*

6 Songs About Roadies

1. "We Are the Road Crew"—Motörhead
2. "Motörhead's Roadie"—the Jazz June
3. "Road Rats"—Alice Cooper
4. "Roadie"—Kung Fu Hula Girl
5. "Roadie Blues"—Paradox
6. "Robber and the Roadie"—Nazareth

Alex Wade of Whitechapel's 10 Things I've Learned While Being a Touring Musician

10. If there's any kind of Mexican catering at the venue, you'd be better off not eating it. You, your band, and your rectum will thank you later when you aren't pulling over every five exits to get to a bathroom.

9. If you drop your pick while playing, just keep playing with your fingers until you can grab a backup pick or the song is over. Don't be that idiot who stops playing and bends over to pick it up during the set.

8. If you have a stomach virus on tour and have constant diarrhea, make sure you're wearing a "manpon" (a few sheets of toilet paper between your butt cheeks); otherwise you might get a little surprise when you strain yourself to headbang.

7. There are no rules on van wars between bands on tour. Anything goes. Anything. As long as you don't blow their van up. That would be a little uncalled for.

6. Keep your distance from other members of your band onstage. A bass headstock to the forehead isn't exactly a pleasant feeling.

5. When you pull up to a house you're staying at and get a bad feeling about it, go with your gut instinct and don't stay there. Otherwise you might be staying at a house with a "puke room," a room where the drunk house members go and puke wherever.

4. Earplugs are your best friend when sleeping in a van with the snoring choir coming from multiple members.

3. Shower shoes aren't necessarily needed for gross showers. Pee on your feet. The ammonia in urine is proven to kill the bacteria that causes athlete's foot. Yes, I'm serious. I'm not just trying to get you to pee on your feet.

2. If a toilet is nowhere around and a number two is on the rise, as long as the number two isn't visible in plain sight, anywhere is game to lay that bad boy, as long as you have wiping material.

1. If you bring a girl back to the van to attempt to get some form of action, be sure you haven't gone too long without a shower; otherwise, she'll get a nice surprising smell when she unzips your pants.

Alex Wade is one of the dual guitarists for Metal Blade recording artists Whitechapel. Formed in February 2006 by Phil Bozeman, Brandon Cagle, and Ben Savage, Knoxville, Tennessee's Whitechapel seamlessly meld death metal, grind, and hardcore to create a blistering brand of modern death metal.

Deal with the Devil: 12 Weird Requests Made in Heavy Metal Contract Riders

1. Korn
Contracts asked for four dimmable lamps ("very, very important—a must"), because the band's dressing rooms must have a certain "vibe."

2. Limp Bizkit
Again with the dimmable lamps.

3. Guns N' Roses
The band had needs . . . and to address those needs, they made sure their dressing room was appropriately stocked with *Penthouse* and *Playboy* magazines, a carton of Dunhills, a carton of Camel filter hard packs, and two cartons of Marlboro reds.

4. Pantera
They requested four aromatherapy candles and some incense, and probably for good reason (see their entry in "Food Demands").

5. AC/DC
During their 2008 tour, the band from the land down under needed live potted trees, "height depending on ceiling."

6. Bon Jovi
The band's dressing room must be "odor free."

7. Rage Against the Machine
Six pairs of boxer shorts (cotton only) and six pairs of tube socks.

8. Aerosmith
On their 1997 tour, the band requested a throat doctor, an internal medicine specialist, an osteo-podiatrist, and a chiropractor. They also made sure that the VIP room was decorated in Eastern Indian style, but "Pakistani compressed towels" were a no-no.

9. Ozzy Osbourne
Contracts called for a doctor capable of giving Ozzy a B-12 shot and the anti-inflammatory Decadron.

10. Poison

The band will not play in a venue that isn't compliant with the Americans with Disabilities Act.

11. Ted Nugent

The Nuge shows his love for Mother Earth not just by killing its game animals but by making sure no Styrofoam cups or plates are used backstage. He also makes damn sure all aluminum cans are recycled.

12. Van Halen

By the time the band hit the road for their 2007–2008 reunion tour they made sure that David Lee Roth's dressing room was "as far away" from those of the Van Halen family as possible, and that venues provided a study room for sixteen-year-old Wolfgang and his tutor. The support act had to make do with "moderate" and yet still "adequate" lighting.

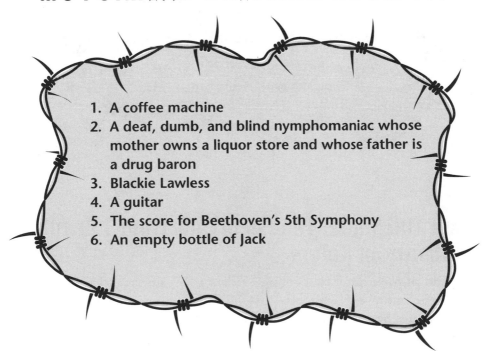

PHIL CAMPBELL OF MOTÖRHEAD'S LIST OF 6 THINGS YOU'LL NEVER SEE IN A MOTÖRHEAD DRESSING ROOM . . .

1. A coffee machine
2. A deaf, dumb, and blind nymphomaniac whose mother owns a liquor store and whose father is a drug baron
3. Blackie Lawless
4. A guitar
5. The score for Beethoven's 5th Symphony
6. An empty bottle of Jack

... AND 11 THINGS THAT ANNOY ME ABOUT HOTELS

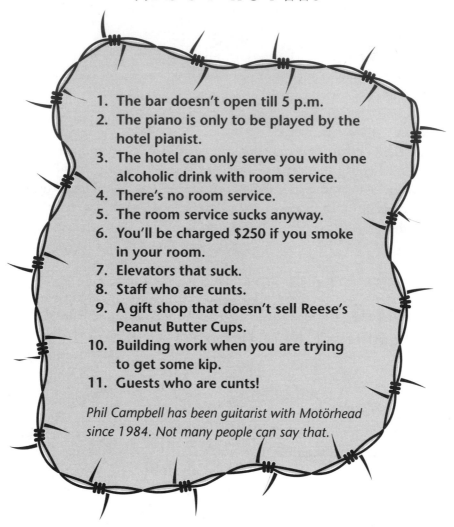

1. The bar doesn't open till 5 p.m.
2. The piano is only to be played by the hotel pianist.
3. The hotel can only serve you with one alcoholic drink with room service.
4. There's no room service.
5. The room service sucks anyway.
6. You'll be charged $250 if you smoke in your room.
7. Elevators that suck.
8. Staff who are cunts.
9. A gift shop that doesn't sell Reese's Peanut Butter Cups.
10. Building work when you are trying to get some kip.
11. Guests who are cunts!

Phil Campbell has been guitarist with Motörhead since 1984. Not many people can say that.

Eat 'Em and Smile: Food Demands from 9 Heavy Metal Contract Riders

In the world of rock 'n' roll tour contract riders, there are the artists (who make the demands), the producers (who relay the demands), and the purchasers (who better make damn sure that everything is carried out to the letter, or your ass is in trouble). Here are some of the more amusing ones.

1. Van Halen

Van Halen's 1982 tour rider is the one that defined the outer limits of rock star indulgence for years to come with its demand for "no brown M&M's." (David Lee Roth later said that clause was only included so they knew people were actually reading the contracts.) Eventually the guys were up to their old tricks again with their demands for Reese's Peanut Butter Cups—individually wrapped, please, and *not* minis and not Reese's Pieces. But they were talkin' Reese's Peanut Butter Cups, so who can blame 'em?

2. Def Leppard

Three members of Def Leppard are vegans, which means that all animal products (from eggs and cheese to honey) are out of the question. They're specific in their contracts about what they want and will even suggest where it can be purchased. And as if you needed any more proof that Def Leppard are the nicest bunch of guys in metal, not only did they keep drummer Rick Allen after he lost his arm, they also make sure that all unused food provided for them backstage is donated to a local homeless shelter.

3. Marilyn Manson

In addition to health-conscious items like Nutrigrain bars, Nature Valley health bars, and Smart Start cereal, Marilyn Manson had producers stock the band bus with tangerine Altoids, four bags of Haribo Gold Gummi Bears, Velveeta mac and cheese, beef jerky, a can of Manwich mix, Lucky Charms and Froot Loops breakfast cereals, Pop-Tarts, and Hostess cakes.

4. Black Sabbath

While Ozzy was happy with smoked salmon and turkey and Tony Iommi had the occasional meal of sea bass or whitefish (unless it was Saturday, when he had two meals of grilled chicken), the rhythm section of Black Sabbath are vegetarian. In fact, bassist Geezer Butler is vegan, so he wants no animal products of any kind in his food. Although where a promoter would find Soya Kass hickory smoke–flavored soy cheese in Middle America is anyone's guess.

5. Aerosmith

When playing on their 1997 tour, Aerosmith requested fresh ears of corn on the cob, "cooked for three minutes only."

6. Metallica

Metallica must have bacon! According to their 2004 tour rider, it was "very important that bacon be served at every meal and during [the] day."

7. Pantera

The band requested an after-performance Taco Bell order of six bean burritos; six bean burritos with green sauce and sour cream; twelve regular tacos; twelve soft-shell tacos; three taco salads; a big bag of hot sauce; and additional takeout orders from KFC, Wendy's, and pizza for the bus.

8. Bon Jovi

On at least one tour Bon Jovi wanted "home-made low-fat chicken noodle soup," served in "appropriate containers." Since they were traveling with twenty vegetarians, "it [was] essential that the vegetarian meals be afforded the same care and attention as general meals." They also made sure that said vegetarians got a "suitable ethnic dish made without meat."

9. Rage Against the Machine

Food requirements: "quality" guacamole and organic, unsalted, raw, macadamia nuts.

Jan Kuehnemund of Vixen's List of 10 Reasons Why I Need My Own Hotel Room on the Road . . .

1. I need the room temperature to be "below zero," year-round.
2. I need *all* the pillows.
3. I set several alarms for wake-up: a cell phone, the TV, a clock radio, and a travel clock. I even call the front desk for a wake-up call. Plus I hit the snooze for at least an hour before actually getting up, which might annoy anyone else sharing the room.
4. I need all the available table, nightstand, and dresser-top space for my traveling snack bar.
5. I often eat sardines as a bedtime snack, which isn't real popular with roommates.
6. I usually get up to visit my snack bar in the middle of the night, and sometimes the rustling of wrappers can be a little noisy.

7. I like to be able to shower whenever I want. One of my dear bandmates, who shall remain nameless, likes to take several showers a day: one before sound check, one after sound check, one or two after the show, one in the morning before breakfast. . . . Need I say more?

8. I sometimes feel the need to play sudoku into the wee hours of the morning.

9. If I see a spider that "gets away" and I can't find it, I'll leave the lights on all night!

10. I love my bandmates, but not in the same hotel room with me!

. . . and the First 12 Things I Do as Soon as I Get In It

1. Turn on the AC as cold as it will go.
2. Lock the door, including dead bolt and chains.
3. Put room key away in special zippered pocket in my purse unless we're in Europe, where you need the room key in wall holder to turn the lights on.
4. Check the lamps and lightbulbs to make sure they all work.
5. Make sure there's enough toilet paper.
6. Get those nasty bedspreads off the beds and throw 'em in a corner.
7. Set up my traveling snack bar and have a snack!
8. After watching a disgusting video about hotel "cleaning" staffs on YouTube, I thoroughly wash the drinking glass. Then I drink about three glasses of (yes) tap water, but only if I'm in the USA!
9. Wipe off and disinfect the dirty TV remote with Handi Wipes. Then I turn on the TV and look for a news channel or VH1.
10. I unlock the door and get a bucket of ice to chill my sardines.
11. Lay out all my belts, stage clothes, and boots so they're ready to jump into, then unpack and line up all toiletries in the bathroom.
12. Check for spiders!

Jan Kuehnemund is a founding member of Vixen, one of the most successful female rock bands in the world. Massive hits like "Edge of a Broken Heart" and "Cryin'" heralded their position in the rock charts—including four singles in Billboard's Hot 100—and made them a permanent fixture on the most popular rock compilation albums of the '90s. The band's latest studio release, Live & Learn, *garnered two 2007 Independent Music Award nominations. Vixen's first ever live CD and DVD,* Live in Sweden, *is scheduled for release in 2009.*

Eric Adams of Manowar's 10 Favorite Metal Cities

1. São Paulo

Great crowds that really love metal music. Monsters of Rock has got to be one of the best metal shows and it's located in São Paulo.

2. Tokyo

I haven't been there in a while, but it's a place I remember well. To look out and witness a sea of wild Japanese fans is hard to forget.

3. Barcelona

This is a city that I'll always return to. I've been there quite a few times and always have a blast. And Spanish wine is nothing to sneeze at, either!

4. Malmö, Sweden

Just because.

5. Kavarna, Bulgaria

Home of the "Metal Mayor" himself. This place really kicks ass. It's grown from just another seaport city, to the rock capital of Bulgaria and soon the world.

6. Dallas

This is the home of some of the most beautiful women in the world. Who wouldn't want to return?

7. Istanbul

If you ever want to be around some metal-starved fans, Istanbul is the place. When you play a show here, the fans go crazy. I love it.

8. London

This is where it all started for me. It was the first major city Manowar played after our second album. Since we headlined for a full house at the Hammersmith Odeon, it has held a treasured place in my heart.

9. Zlín, Czech Republic

Other than the grueling ride from the airport, everything else about this city is pretty cool. The promoter always makes sure everything is top shelf and that means a great show.

10. Germany

I know, I know. Germany isn't a city. But as far as I'm concerned, Germany is a metal nation full of metal cities with crazy metal fans. I have to admit, if I were to live in any other country in the world, Germany would be my choice.

Eric Adams has been the lead singer of Manowar since 1980. He's also an accomplished bow hunter who produced and appears in the DVD Wild Life and Wild Times. *He is represented by Metal Circle Music and regularly appears at their Metal Circle Festival in Germany.*

Bob Gorman [a.k.a. Muzzle Slave] of Gwar's 10 Weirdest Places Gwar Have Performed

1. A slaughterhouse in Cologne, Germany

When our tour bus pulled up to this gig, the part of the building we were facing looked abandoned and ready to collapse. Both turned out to be true. Once we gained access to the facility, we realized that the building we were to perform in was once part of a complex of abandoned slaughterhouses. Later several of us broke into another, locked, building in the complex. In an office we found photographs of the complex from the '50s. The photographs showed Russian officers and workers in radioactive jumpsuits running a Geiger counter over live cattle. As the day progressed, we saw men in lab coats walking between the other buildings. It hadn't occurred to us until then that we were playing one end of a slaughterhouse that was still in use. When the show started and the first of our stage blood hit the dirty floor, the smell that arose was like nothing I had ever smelled before. Pretty gross, even by Gwar standards. We always refer back to this show as "Cowschwitz."

2. A Howard Johnson's lobby in Calgary, Alberta, Canada

This gig was a particular low as far as touring goes. Heading east through Canada at the end of a winter tour, one by one we began succumbing to a mysterious illness. Then a week of dates fell through. This was the last show I remember before we all said, "Fuck it, let's go home." I can't remember where the musicians got dressed, because there was no dressing room. I do remember that us performers changed costumes in a mop closet. To get onstage we had to go out a back door, and then across a parking lot (it was snowing that night). Then we had to open a double barn door right behind Brad, our drummer. There were no steps, so in costume we had to hoist ourselves onto the stage, get killed, then travel back through the snow (covered in blood) to the mop closet.

184

3. A parking garage in Pontiac, Michigan

This show started out pretty well, considering. Gwar has never had a lot of luck playing outdoors, but at first this show seemed an exception. The production was professional, and even though getting covered in fake blood outside . . . at night . . . in the winter . . . is not your first choice, the other factors seemed to outweigh the inconvenience. Things changed quickly. There were stairs in front of the entire stage that restricted things. Quite simply put, we were too far away and the blood wasn't hitting the audience, and they really couldn't see the band too well. As the show progressed, several members of the band playing victims ventured out onto the steps to try and get blood on the crowd. This seemed to only enrage the crowd more and they proceeded to tear the feeder cable to the sound booth in two. Our adventurous bass player got on the stairs too close to the crowd and was bulldogged by a huge goon. A lot of us started punching him and he finally let go, but not before ripping the bass player's helmet in two. We finished the show as the security quelled the near-riot crowd. They're animals in Michigan.

4. An abandoned airport in Munich, Germany

From what I could gather, Munich had built a brand-new airport miles away. While preparing to tear down the old airport, it was squatted and turned into a series of nightclubs. It was really like a postapocalyptic movie, and we had an entire terminal as a dressing room.

5. A skating rink in Boise, Idaho

While we were loading in the back of this venue, the front was still open for business. "Skateworld" was having one of those specific skate days for mainly really young kids. I remember Hunter, who had always been an avid roller skater, put his skates on and got out there with these little kids. I was really weird seeing this forty-year-old in tattered jean shorts doing 70's style skate moves in between nine-year-olds.

6. A skateboard ramp in Cedarcrest, Virginia

In 1989, Gwar was still touring in a 1974 International Harvester school bus. It had stickers, graffiti, skulls, a pair of steer horns, and most importantly a giant "GWAR" painted above the windshield. When we pulled up to the gate that led to the skate ramp, the owner of the establishment, (the man who had booked Gwar to play) came out. He proceeded to pull a gun out of his pants. Waving the gun around, he approached the bus and said, "Who are you guys?" The rest of the night went in a similar fashion.

7. A state fair bird building in Salt Lake City, Utah

The "Fowl Friends Building" pretty much says it all. About a year later on an *America's Most Wanted* special on hate-edge, I found out a Gwar fan had been stabbed to death at a 7-Eleven a couple of blocks away after that show.

8. A bowling alley in Omaha, Nebraska

Tiny stage, crappy show. We did however get in costume and bowl a full game before we played.

9. An abandoned tuberculosis asylum in Louisville, Kentucky

As the rock industry, and Gwar, got more professional, the weird stuff really trailed off, but this show was a return to the golden days of yesteryear—and complete chaos. First off, the capacity of the show was set at three thousand. The promoter sold e-tickets, and apparently many people printed doubles and sold them. To make matters worse, the asylum was set in a remote wooded area, and hundreds of other people walked through the woods to gain access. The result was such severe overcrowding that there were not enough bathrooms, water, tents, you name it. The security barely kept the local police from shutting the show down twice. In the end the owners lost the right to hold any more shows at the facility and the promoter ran off with the receipts and some of the money.

10. An abandoned underground highway tunnel in Stuttgart, Germany

This gig went really well. At first it seemed strange we were playing in an underground concrete tube. Later in the day I retreated further and further underground. It seems this concrete tube was actually built as a highway tunnel. There was an active highway tunnel fairly close, so perhaps this was a sister tunnel that was never opened. I finally walked far enough and emerged on the other side of a mountain, where the opening was blocked by an enormous metal grate. Returning to the club, I was pretty disappointed there were no Nazi treasures buried there.

Bob Gorman does what Gwar tells him to do.

17 Metalheads' Stage Names and How They Got Them

1. Lemmy Kilmister

The name came from his habit of borrowing money, as in, "Lemme borrow a fiver."

2. Geezer Butler

According to the man himself, "I had three brothers in the army and, in that time, we called each other 'Geezer.' It was the thing to do. I'd go around school calling people 'Geezer.' But in the end I got cursed with the nickname from my brothers calling me that so much."

3. John 5 (Marilyn Manson)

Born John Lowery, he was rechristened John 5 the day he joined Marilyn Manson.

4. Bumblefoot (Guns N' Roses)

While helping his wife study to become a veterinarian, Ron Thal learned that bumblefoot is a bacterial disease birds can get in their feet.

5. Gene Simmons (Kiss)

Born in Israel as Chaim Witz, the bassist had his name Americanized to Gene Klein in his youth. His stage name probably comes from rockabilly star "Jumpin'" Gene Simmons, who had a minor hit with the song "Haunted House" in the early '60s.

6. Paul Stanley (Kiss)

The Starchild's real name is Stanley Eisen, and he chose the name Paul as a member of Wicked Lester in the early '70s.

7. Ace Frehley (Kiss)

When Paul Frehley was told by Gene Simmons and Paul Stanley that there wasn't enough room in Kiss for two Pauls, Frehley reverted to the nickname he earned as a teen with his ability to get dates for his friends.

8. Peter Criss (Kiss)

The Catman was born Peter Crisscoula.

9. W. Axl Rose

The former William Bruce Rose was once in a band called Axl.

10. Slash

"It was a nickname that [actor] Seymour Cassel used to call me," recalls the artist formerly known as Saul Hudson. "I'm good friends with his son, Matt, so I used to hang out over at their house and he always used to call me Slash. Basically, he says it was because I was always in a hurry and I was always scheming, I was always hustling, this and that. He always saw me on the go, on the fly. So he used to call me Slash and it just stuck. My friends started calling me that and it just became a permanent nickname."

11. Dimebag Darrell
Darrell Lance Abbott's nickname used to be Diamond Darrell, but when Pantera started going for a rougher-edged sound, he changed it to Dimebag.

12. The Great Kat
The English-born neo-classical guitar shred goddess's first name is Katherine.

13. Percy
Robert Plant was being razzed by his fellow Zeppelins while they were watching television, when John Paul Jones had mentioned Percy Thrower, host of a popular gardening show in the U.K. Jones asked how a show about watching plants grow could be interesting, and Jimmy Page said, "That's what *we* do, watch Plant grow!"

14. Bonzo
The heavy-handed Led Zeppelin drummer was nicknamed Bonzo after a dog in a British comic strip created by artist George Studdy in the '20s.

15. John Paul Jones
When John Baldwin was a session musician in England in the '60s, producer Andrew Loog Oldham suggested the name, remembering it from the title of a movie about the Revolutionary War naval officer he'd seen on a poster in France.

16. Sebastian Bach
The Canadian metal star's birth name was Sebastian Bierk.

17. Buckethead
Uh, because he wears a bucket on his head . . .

Evan Seinfeld of Biohazard's Top 5 Famous Heavy Metal Cars, Top 5 Factory Muscle Cars, and One Honorable Mention

Top 5 Factory Muscle Cars
1. 1970 Chevy Chevelle SS LS6
2. 1971 Plymouth Hemi Cuda
3. 1970 Buick GSX stage 1
4. 1966 Pontiac Bonneville
5. 1961 Cadillac Coupe Deville triple black

Top 5 Famous Heavy Metal Cars
1. Mad Max—the last of the V8 interceptors
2. The Batmobile, built by Barris Kustoms
3. The '68 440 Dodge Charger RT from the movie *Bullit*, driven by Steve McQueen
4. The Deathmobile from *Animal House*
5. Sylvester Stallone's chopped Merc from *Cobra*.

Honorable Mention
Cadzilla, owned by Billy Gibbons of ZZ Top, built by Boyd Coddington

As a founding member, lead singer, and bassist of the groundbreaking social hardcore band Biohazard, Evan Seinfeld led the Brooklyn-bred rockers to multiplatinum status and critical acclaim for the past twenty years, releasing ten albums and reaching nearly 4 million units sold worldwide without a single spin on commercial radio. He has conquered the worlds of music, television, film, and photography—both in the mainstream and triple-X playing fields—and has only just begun to fulfill his creative dreams.

WHOLE LOTTA LISTS

Special When Lit: Aaron Lefkove's 7 Wonders of Heavy Metal Pinball

1. Kiss (Bally, 1978)

The quintessential heavy metal pinball machine, this early table would actually play the melody to "Rock and Roll All Nite" every time a ball was put into play. Though it lacks the bells and whistles of later machines, the Kiss table was the first and still ranks as one of the best. Kiss pinball was later reprised as a video game for the Sony PlayStation.

2. Guns N' Roses (Data East, 1994)

The mid-'90s may have been the beginning of a very long lull for GNR, but even with the band in disarray Data East managed to pull it together for what is certainly a high water mark so far as metal pinball machines are concerned. The band's full classic lineup (including Izzy Stradlin and Dizzy Reed!) are depicted amongst an intense playfield that includes numerous ramps, bumpers, tubes, lighted guitars, rattlesnake tails, a back glass that depicts the original skulls-on-a-cross design, and pumping hi-fi music.

3. Heavy Metal Meltdown (Bally Midway, 1987)

Perhaps the first metal-sploitation machine, Heavy Metal Meltdown includes more cliché hesher metal imagery than Sabbath had drummers. The playfield design looks like a cross between *Pyromania* and David Lee Roth–era Van Halen stage sets. The machine has a boom box on top that blasts a crunchy riff with every new move you make.

4. Baywatch (Sega, 1995)

Baywatch the show may not be very metal—David Hasselhoff's solo records are anything but—however, vixen star Pam Anderson, who figures prominently on this table, has a litany of former lovers, including Poison's Bret Michaels, Mötley Crüe's Tommy Lee, and Kid Rock, that reads like a stellar lineup at Castle Donington.

5. Crüe Ball (Sega, 1992)

Technically this wasn't an actual machine, but the Crüe did have their own pinball video game for Sega Genesis. The 1992 game cartridge included versions of three of the band's songs: "Dr. Feelgood," "Live Wire," and "Home Sweet Home."

6. Iron Maiden (Williams, 2005)

No other band in the metal arena lends itself more perfectly to a pinball machine than Iron Maiden and their Derek Riggs–designed mascot, Eddie the Head. The back glass is a stark portrayal of Eddie as he first appeared on Maiden's debut LP. The playfield is rife with Eddie in a number of different incarnations: as the Philip K. Dick–inspired cyborg of *Somewhere in Time*; as *Phantom of the Opera*'s organ grinder; bursting out of the grave à la *No Prayer for the Dying*; as the patriotic British soldier from *The Trooper*; and, of course, as the bat off of the *Live at Donington* cover.

7. Heavy Metal (Rowamet, 1981)

This machine was produced to promote the animated movie *Heavy Metal*, which itself was an offshoot of the sci-fi comic book of the same name. The back glass depicts the classic "Lita Ford Valkyrie-riding bird dragon" design that appeared on the movie poster.

Backbeat wunderkind Aaron Lefkove has been waiting since Iron Maiden's Paul Dianno era for his love of pinball and heavy metal to come to a crossroads.

20 Heavy Metal Party Bands with Fucking Awesome Names

1. Atomic Mullet
2. Mullethead
3. Hairem
4. Hairbangers Ball
5. Mr. Tripod
6. Scum Gumbo

7. That 80s Hair Band
8. Glam R Us
9. Hamyzfear
10. Butterface
11. The Final Crap from Hell
12. AMPutee
13. 80's Proof
14. Riff Raff
15. InHalen (VH cover band)
16. Sunset Stripped
17. AB/CD (AC/DC cover band)
18. BC/DC (AC/DC cover band)
19. Seedy/DC
20. Ducks Can Groove (Swedish Hendrix cover band

Brandon Patton of Echoes of Eternity's 3 Reasons Why Being a Professional Musician Sucks

1. You're always broke.

We've all heard about the stereotypical financially struggling musician. It's true, though. Just go to a pawnshop and look at all the music gear they got from some dude who sold his axe to put some gas in his piece-of-shit car and buy a twelve-pack. The musicians I know are all working shitty part-time jobs just so they can drop everything at a moment's notice and go on tour and live in a fucking van with four other smelly dudes. Sweet.

2. You move your fingers around on a piece of wood for a living.

I'm a guitarist, so that means I am hedging all my bets on the hope that one day I'll be able to get by in this world by strapping a piece of wood on and moving my fingers around. Great idea.

3. It's like a bad meth habit.

Think about it. The only thing that makes you feel completely alive simultaneously sucks the life out of you. You try to walk away and you can't. You want to drop it and go get a "real" job and you don't. And being a musician doesn't exactly have a stellar compensation package, a 401(k), or a great health-care plan, so you may end up with no teeth, prematurely old from the road and all that greasy pizza every fucking venue gives you. Yup, being a musician is just like being that tweaker dude who rides around on a bike huffing spray paint and going from door to door trying to sell a fucking chain saw so he can get a few bucks and spend the next three days grinding his teeth and reassembling shredded documents for an identity-theft ring. Okay, maybe it's not that fucking bad.

Brandon Patton is the guitarist and founding member of Echoes of Eternity, who are signed to Nuclear Blast Records.

Gimme Some Money: 12 Heavy Metal Pitchmen and What They Shill

1. Slash (Velvet Revolver)
Black Death Vodka
Volkswagen
John Varvatos clothing

2. Nigel Tufnel (Spinal Tap)
Volkswagen
National Geographic *Stonehenge Rediscovered* television show

3. Alice Cooper
Marriott Residence Inn
Callaway Golf Clubs
Bridgestone Tires
Staples
John Varvatos
Fisher 24 CD changer
Miller beer
21st Century Insurance
CompUSA
TV-Shop
Sky Digital Plus
Longhorn Steakhouse

4. Lemmy Kilmister (Motörhead)
Kit Kat bars

5. Peter Frampton (Humble Pie)
Geico auto insurance

6. Sixx A.M.
Wal-Mart

7. Steven Tyler
Sony Cybershot camera
Got Milk? (print ad)
The Gap (with Joe Perry)

8. Spinal Tap
IBM

9. Ozzy Osbourne
Samsung Propel phone
World of Warcraft video game
Pepsi Twist

10. Dee Snider
Snider has done voice-over work for Pizza Hut, NYS Lotto, and MSNBC.

11. Bret Michaels
Time-Life's *Hard and Heavy* CD subscription series

12. Ted Nugent
Eveready batteries

But Wait! There's More! 32 Great Moments in Kiss Merchandising

After ringing the opening bell at the New York Stock Exchange, Gene Simmons told financial channel CNBC there are more than three thousand pieces of officially licensed Kiss merchandise. Here's about .01 percent of what's available.

1. Bally pinball machines
2. "Stuck on Chuck" decals (to cover the stars on your Chuck Taylor sneakers)
3. Automobile air fresheners
4. Coffins
5. Condoms
6. Footballs
7. Baby bibs
8. *Destroyer* diaper bags
9. DVD board games
10. Toddler T-shirts (with picture of Kiss as teddy bears)
11. Cycling skins/socks/shorts
12. Arm warmers
13. Street bike helmets

14. "Hotter than Hell" kitchen aprons
15. Demon ducks (rubber ducks with Gene's head)
16. Puzzle cubes (a Rubik's Cube with the band's faces)
17. Pool sticks and cue balls (each item sold separately)
18. Checkers sets
19. Drinking dice sets
20. Silver coins
21. Personal checks
22. Collectible wine
23. Box Set guitar cases
24. Christmas ornaments
25. Lip balm
26. Toothbrushes
27. Bar stools
28. Portable iPod speakers
29. Golf club covers
30. Fragrances
31. Pez dispensers
32. I-Dogs

Stay with Me, Baby: Lita Ford and Jim Gillette's 12 Ways to Make a Metal Marriage Last

1. Marry the right person! That might sound silly, but think about it.
2. Love them with all your heart. Nothing is more important than your mate. They come first, without exception (no pun intended)! If anyone or anything is causing turbulence, get rid of it.
3. Have lots and lots of great, adventurous sex. So many marriages end because of sex. If you're getting all the sex you want at home, why would you look somewhere else? A lot of this might sound like common sense, but if people used common sense today, the divorce rate wouldn't be so high!
4. Dress up in bondage clothes. For those on a budget, try nipple rings and high heels.
5. Spank your husband regularly; he'll probably love it! If that doesn't work, smack him upside the head with a frying pan!
6. Learn the Kama Sutra or suck a toe. Preferably the big one.

7. Have lots of sex toys and use them regularly. Don't forget to sterilize!

8. Tell your significant other how much you love them at least a hundred times a day. We try to hit five hundred!

9. Divorce is not an option. Marriage is till death do you part. And no, that does not mean you can kill them!

10. Tattoo their name, picture, anniversary date, etc., on your body!

11. Worship them for being the god or goddess that they are, even if they are a tad bit overweight!

12. Always have their best interest at heart, not your own. Every decision you make should be for the benefit of your family. You are husband and wife: two bodies with one soul. Live and breathe for your partner, and don't forget to wipe from front to back to avoid any bacterial infections!

Guitar goddess Lita Ford and former Nitro front man Jim Gillette have been married for fifteen years and have two children. They are very much in love.

Hail, Seitan! 30 Heavy Metal Vegans and Vegetarians

These metal warriors are now, or once were, vegetarians or vegans, for a variety of reasons.

1. Kirk Hammett (Metallica)
2. Rick Allen (Def Leppard)
3. Phil Collen (Def Leppard)
4. Vivian Campbell (Def Leppard)
5. Rob Zombie
6. Rick Rubin
7. Tim Commerford (Rage Against the Machine)
8. Serj Tankian (System of a Down)
9. Antonietta Scilipoti (Evanfast)
10. Anthony Kiedis (Red Hot Chili Peppers)
11. Fallon Bowman (Kittie)
12. Kristine Liv (Theatre of Tragedy)
13. Martin Walkyier (Sabbat, Skyclad)
14. Gaahl (Gorgoroth)
15. Andrew Vowles (Massive Attack)
16. Jeff Walker (Carcass, Blackstar Rising)

17. Ken Owen (Carcass, Blackstar Rising)
18. Bill Steer (Napalm Death, Carcass, Firebird)
19. Eddie Jackson, (Queensrÿche)
20. Geoff Tate (Queensrÿche)
21. Bill Ward (Black Sabbath)
22. Geezer Butler (vegan since he was eight years old)
23. Dan Briggs (Between the Buried & Me)
24. Paul Waggoner (Between the Buried & Me)
25. Tommy Rogers (Between the Buried & Me)
26. Dweezil Zappa
27. Steve Vai
28. Rikki Rockett (Poison; vegan)
29. Kevin Ridley (Skyclad)
30. Noel Marbais (Falling Elbow)

Six Feet Over: 34 Towering Metalheads

1. Geezer Butler (Black Sabbath) 6´
2. Steve Vai 6´
3. David Lee Roth (Van Halen) 6´
4. Alex Van Halen (Van Halen) 6´
5. Dave Mustaine (Megadeth) 6´
6. Tom Hamilton (Aerosmith) 6´ 1˝
7. Don Dokken (Dokken) 6´ 1˝
8. Jani Lane (Warrant) 6´ 1˝
9. Robert Plant (Led Zeppelin) 6´ 1˝
10. Jerry Cantrell (Alice in Chains) 6´ 1˝
11. James Hetfield (Metallica) 6´ 1˝
12. Ace Frehley (Kiss) 6´ 1˝
13. Serj Tankian (System of a Down) 6´ 1˝
14. Nikki Sixx (Mötley Crüe) 6´ 1˝
15. Marilyn Manson 6´ 1˝
16. Joe Elliot (Def Leppard) 6´ 1½˝
17. Jonathan Davis (Korn) 6´ 2˝
18. James "Munky" Shaffer (Korn) 6´ 2˝
19. Marco Hiatala (Nightwish) 6´ 2˝
20. Tony Iommi (Black Sabbath) 6´ 2˝

21. Burton C. Bel (Fear Factory) 6´ 2˝
22. Brian May (Queen) 6´ 2˝
23. Ian Gillan (Deep Purple) 6´ 2˝
24. Gene Simmons (Kiss) 6´ 2˝
25. Tommy Lee (Mötley Crüe) 6´ 2½˝
26. Yngwie J. Malmsteen 6´ 3˝
27. Rob Ourdon (Linkin Park) 6´ 4˝
28. Sebastian Bach 6´ 4˝
29. Neal Peart (Rush) 6´ 4˝
30. Blackie Lawless (W.A.S.P.) 6´ 4˝
31. Danny Carey (Tool) 6´ 5˝
32. Page Hamilton (Helmet) 6´ 5˝
33. Chris Holmes (W.A.S.P.) 6´ 5˝
34. Pete Steele (Type O Negative) 6´ 8˝

LITTLE BIG MEN: 9 METALHEADS WHO ARE 5´6˝ OR UNDER

1. **King Diamond (Mercyful Fate) 5' 6"**
2. **Bruce Dickinson (Iron Maiden) 5' 6"**
3. **Dani Filth (Cradle of Filth) 5' 5"**
4. **Scott Ian (Anthrax) 5' 5½"**
5. **Klaus Meine (Scorpions) 5' 5"**
6. **Ronnie James Dio (Heaven and Hell) 5' 4"**
7. **Glenn Danzig (Danzig) 5' 3"**
8. **Malcolm Young (AC/DC) 5' 3"**
9. **Angus Young (AC/DC) 5' 2"**

20 Metalheads Who Should *Never* Wear Spandex, Corsets, or Fishnet . . .

1. Bill Ward (Black Sabbath)
2. Fred Durst (Limp Bizkit)
3. Glenn Danzig (Danzig)
4. Ronnie James Dio (Heaven and Hell)
5. Rick Allen (Def Leppard)
6. Peter Steele (Type O Negative)
7. Dee Snider (Twistes Sister)
8. Angus Young (AC/DC)
9. Evil J (Otep)
10. Kerry King (Slayer)
11. Zakk Wylde (Black Label Society)
12. Phil Anselmo (Pantera)
13. Billy Milano (S.O.D.)
14. Vinnie Abbott (Damageplan)
15. Evan Seinfeld (Biohazard)
16. Geddy Lee (Rush)
17. King Diamond
18. Jimmy Page (Led Zeppelin)
19. James Hetfield (Metallica)
20. Lemmy Kilmister (Motörhead, although it would be funny, once)

. . . and 20 Who Should *Never* Leave Home Without Them

1. Lita Ford
2. The Great Kat
3. Doro Pesch
4. Floor Jansen (After Forever)
5. Maria Brink (In This Moment)
6. Tarja Turunen (ex-Nightwish)
7. Magali Luyten (Beautiful Sin)
8. Sharon den Adel (Within Temptation)
9. Simone Simons (Epica)
10. Dawn Desireé
11. Catherine Paulsen (Trail of Tears)
12. Veronica Freeman (Benedictum)
13. Quinn Weng (Serpahim)

14. Tanja Lainio (Lullacry)
15. Marjan Welman (Autumn)
16. Morena Rozzi (Macbeth)
17. Helen Vogt (Flowing Tears)
18. Stephanie Luzie (Atargatis)
19. Julie Kiss (To-Mera)
20. Anette Olson (Nightwish)

Otep Shamaya's 10 Most Recently Read Books

1. *Armageddon in Retrospect* by Kurt Vonnegut
2. *Fear & Loathing on the Campaign Trail 1972* by Hunter S. Thompson
3. *An Incomplete Education Vol. 3* by Judy Jones & William Wilson
4. *Anthem* by Ayn Rand
5. *A People's History of the United States* by Howard Zinn
6. *Imperial America: Reflections on the United States of Amnesia* by Gore Vidal
7. *Kingdom of Fear* by Hunter S. Thompson
8. *God Is Dead* by Ron Currie, Jr.
9. *A Season in Hell* by Arthur Rimbaud
10. *The Complete Poetry & Prose of William Blake*

Otep Shamaya is lead singer of Otep, which formed in 2000 and has released four albums. She is the author of two books, Caught Screaming *and* Little Sins, *and the spoken-word EP titled* Wurd Becomes Flesh, *and has appeared on HBO's* Def Poetry.

4 Metalheads Who Have Done Musical Theater

1. Sebastian Bach (Skid Row)
Bas has been in several musicals, playing characters from the lead in *Jekyll & Hyde* to Riff Raff in *The Rocky Horror Show* and Jesus in *Jesus Christ Superstar*.

2. Paul Stanley (Kiss)
Paul took the lead role in *Phantom of the Opera* for a run in Toronto in 1999.

3. Corey Glover (Living Colour)
Glover played Judas in *Jesus Christ Superstar*.

4. Gary Cherone (Extreme, Van Halen)
Cherone also played Judas in *Jesus Christ Superstar*.

The Good, the Bad, and the Ugly: Alex Mitchell of Circus of Power's Top 3 Metal Moments

1. The Good

I was down in Florida driving through Everglades City, a place that makes the movie *Deliverance* look like Sesame Street, when a 1970 root beer–colored Nova pulled up beside me at a light. Sabbath's "Sweet Leaf" was blasting from inside. The girl in the passenger seat had one foot on the dash and one out the window (she had very sexy tootsies). She looked over at me and blew some grayish-blue Marlboro smoke in my direction. Both she and the driver, whom I figured was her boyfriend, had matching blond mullets. He saw me checking out his runaway girlfriend, so he leaned forward and shot me a bird. She laughed and then winked at me. She was as sexy as a hornet. When they peeled out, I saw the white letters that had been stuck on the back of their car: "True Love Rocks Hard."

2. The Bad

When I first moved to New York I was living at my friend's uncle's house in Queens; it was real *Welcome Back, Kotter*–type shit and I loved it. One night I walked down to the corner to get some Chinese food and saw some metal kids hanging out inside. They were classic Queens metalheads with leather jackets, denim vests, jeans, white sneakers. They had a boom box playing some Judas Priest and were talking about Halford in thick Queens accents. One kid said, "Yo, that dude is bad lookin'."

His friend said, "Yeah, I saw them live and he had this jacket on with like, 10,000 studs on it."

I couldn't resist it, so I said, "You know he's gay, right?"

The room suddenly went silent. The music stopped. They all stared at me in disbelief. Even the Chinese guy spinning chicken in the wok looked up.

One of the metal kids said, "Halfudd, gay? Whattya mean?"

I assessed the situation. I wasn't being threatened physically but I ran the risk of shitting on someone's dream, so I backed up. "Well, that's what I heard, but, I'm sure it's bullshit, right?"

They all looked at each other and then at me. "Yeah, that's bullshit. Halford rocks!"

He turned the boom box back up, ole Halford was screaming for vengeance, the Chinese guy went back to spinning the chicken, and at that moment I wished I was as metal as they were.

3. The Ugly

I was at an after hours party at this loft in the Big Apple when I ran into Joey Ramone, who was almost as fucked up as I was. There was probably about twenty people there, sitting around talking or making out, and there was a band playing on a makeshift stage. They started playing "Highway Star" by Deep Purple, so Joey and I stumbled onto the stage and grabbed some mics. I don't know who was worse, him or me, but it sounded like two retards trying to sing (no offense to the developmentally challenged). Halfway through the song Joey fell off the stage and I puked all over the mic. The funny thing was, no one was even watching us, so no one even noticed. But hey, that was New York.

Singer, artist, and writer Alex Mitchell is former front man for Circus of Power and author of the books Working Class Superstar *and* Life Is a Phantom Kmart Horse Starting Up in the Middle of the Night.

Heavy Metal Parking Lot Director Jeff Krulik's 12 Movies with a Metal Attitude

1–3. *Planet of the Apes, The Omega Man,* and *Soylent Green*

Classics of late-'60s, early-'70s off-the-chart nihilistic sci-fi. Abandon all hope, all ye who enter here. No one can dispute that Chuck Heston was at his antihero finest back then, especially in *Planet of the Apes* ("Get your stinkin' paws off of me, you damn dirty ape!"). Growing up in Bowie, Maryland, we had a next-door neighbor, Mr. Clese, who took a bunch of neighborhood kids to see *Planet of the Apes* at a local matinee. I must have been seven or eight years old. Talk about warping a kid for life!

4. *Animal House*

Animal House is the ultimate anti-authority, nonconformist film comedy. It's David vs. Goliath, it's good vs. evil, it's God vs. the devil (literally in one classic scene), and it's defined by one of the greatest comic actors of all time. Belushi got big props from the D.C. punk rock crowd for inviting a bunch of punks for Fear's 1981 appearance on *Saturday Night Live*. If he'd lived long enough, you can guarantee he would have been headbanging and air-shredding.

5–6. *Female Trouble* and *Desperate Living*

Two of my favorite John Waters films, both burned into my brain when I saw them on a double bill at the Biograph Theater in D.C. I knew I'd get along fine with my co-director John Heyn the first time I met him, especially when I found out that he worked as a production assistant on *Polyester*. We're both greatly influenced by John Waters, and he was one of the first people we sent a copy of *Heavy Metal Parking Lot* in 1986. He thanked us with a postcard saying that the people in it "gave him the creeps."

7–8. *Night of the Living Dead* and *Dawn of the Dead*

The quintessential zombie carnage horror films, from director George Romero. *Night* was a bold and revolutionary statement filmed in black-and-white. People had never seen anything like it. To be able to top *NOLD* seemed impossible, but the only one who could possibly do it was Romero himself. Those two zombie films are the blueprint, and they have rarely been equaled. I saw them both as midnight films: *Night* when I was just a kid in the mid-'70s (it scared the crap out of me), and *Dawn* when I was in college, at a packed student union theater. Seeing that kind of film with a sold-out, amped-up audience was almost a religious experience. It was unforgettable.

9. *The Road Warrior*

An astonishing sequel to an astonishing film, and one that defined the genre of post-apocalypse filmmaking. Every frame of that end-of-the-world film has a heavy metal feeling: menace, dread, adrenaline with an impeccable sense of humor and over-the-top characters who fill the screen from start to finish. John's a huge fan of *Mad Max* and once went to an advance screening of *The Road Warrior* where the crowd gave it a ten-minute standing ovation.

10. *Beyond the Valley of the Dolls*

I know I sound like a broken (heavy metal) record saying, "There'll never be another film like it," but in the case of *Beyond the Valley of the Dolls*, it's true. I finally got to see this film at a University of Maryland midnight screening right after I graduated college. I had heard it was a great cult film and blah blah blah, and I was jaded enough to say, "Okay, show me what you got." Well, I sat there slack-jawed until halfway through, when I whispered to my friend, "I've never seen anything like this." His two-word response: "Just wait!" *Beyond the Valley of the Dolls* is the film definition of "over-the-top." Accept no substitutes.

11. *The Stoned Age*

If we made a narrative feature of *Heavy Metal Parking Lot*, I've always envisioned it to be like *The Stoned Age*, a somewhat forgotten paean to the lost days of youth, set during a night in the life of two partying late-'70s teenagers. It stars Grace Slick's daughter China and features a hilarious scene goofing on the laser show at a Blue Öyster Cult concert. I discovered this film on cable one night and never forgot it. I even bought a VHS copy recently in a cutout bin at a local drugstore. Ever the fanboy, I've still got the tape mint and sealed in shrink-wrap. I just needed to own it.

12. *Salò, or The 120 Days of Sodom*

I had to watch this film on a bootleg video tape borrowed from a collector friend; back in the 1980s, films like this were impossible to see unless you bought or traded for bootlegs of rare laser discs. *Salò* is one of the most twisted, unbelievable films of all time, a grim orgy of fascist torture, sexual weirdness, and eating excrement. I'm not making this up. The Marquis de Sade did!

In 1986, Jeff Krulik and John Heyn filmed the cult classic Heavy Metal Parking Lot *with borrowed TV equipment at a Judas Priest concert in Largo, Maryland, in two hours. Almost twenty-five years later, their fifteen-minute documentary is more popular than ever. It's taught in film classes, has spawned several sequels and a television series, and is considered one of the top rockumentaries of all time. Jeff and John continue to work in film, television, and video from their Washington, D.C., and suburban Maryland homes, respectively.*

21 HAIR METAL VIDEO FASHION TIPS

1. Spandex
2. Striped Spandex (diagonal or vertical only!)
3. Crosses
4. Turquoise rings
5. Bolo ties
6. Leopard print
7. Zebra print
8. Snakeskin boots
9. A suede jacket
10. Fringe
11. A ruffled shirt
12. Wristbands ('cuz you'll be sweating)
13. Sunglasses
14. Leather
15. Studs (the more, the studlier)
16. A denim vest
17. A motorcycle jacket (unless you've ever really been on a bike)
18. A duster jacket (unless you've actually been out West)
19. A cowboy hat (unless you're really a cowboy)
20. A kamikaze headband (unless you're really Japanese)
21. Bandanas (unless you have hair)

36 Hair Metal Video Clichés

1. Monster shot of an adoring crowd in a sold-out arena
2. Shot of lonesome band members staring out the tour bus window wondering, "Does life on the road ever end?"
3. Girl in adoring crowd on boyfriend's shoulders, showing her tits in slow motion. Freeze frames just before the good part
4. Slow-motion footage of band member autographing a young fan's tits
5. Grainy, black-and-white footage of band members backstage collapsing in a big, comfy chair with a bottle of Jack
6. More tits
7. Someone in a straitjacket (if you can't get a stripper, use the lead singer)
8. Smoke
9. Flames
10. Skulls
11. Flaming skulls in clouds of smoke
12. Pentagrams
13. Satan
14. One shot each of the bass player and drummer
15. The singer doing ballet kicks
16. A badass guitar solo
17. A poignant piano interlude
18. The singer singing in a rainstorm
19. Tits getting wet
20. Lots of hair
21. Lots of hats
22. Lots of tats
23. Lots of tits with tats
24. A train kicking up dust along a lonesome horizon
25. Strippers
26. Porn stars
27. Primping in front of a mirror putting on hair spray and makeup (the band, not the strippers and porn stars)
28. Band sitting in manager's office, taking care of business
29. The band in the studio late at night, putting out cigarette in an overflowing ashtray while the singer does vocal takes
30. The band accepting a platinum record
31. Band walking into a record store and going to their own record bin (for '80s bands only)

32. Band member falling into nightclub booth surrounded by fans and flunkies
33. Band member touching foreheads with sexy girlfriend-type
34. Limo driving off onto Sunset Strip at night
35. Hotel room door shutting, then reopening so band member can hang "Do Not Disturb" sign on door handle
36. Band member pointing at the camera and giving a sly little wink

The *Colbert Report*'s Resident Rocker Jason Baker's 6 Incidences of Heavy Metal Hair Loss

1. David Lee Roth (Van Halen)

Ahh, what can I say about Diamond Dave? He was the ringleader of one of the biggest bands ever. He took his appearance/persona seriously. He was a walking, talking self-promoter. And he was really good at it. Somewhere along the journey, though, he lost his way and cut (or lost) his hair. I'll never understand, but I will admit that it probably wasn't entirely Dave's idea. Is this the reason he and the band went their separate ways? I doubt it, but he still shouldn't have cut his hair.

2. Tommy Lee (Mötley Crüe)

I think Tommy grew his hair because he read some heavy metal handbook that said he should. After his years of great success, he didn't think he needed it any more. Are you kidding me? That is not heavy metal. Sorry.

3. Chris Cornell (Soundgarden)

I think this guy has one of the most powerful voices around, and he had badass long black hair. A serious combination. But he chopped his hair a while ago, and now he's been working with Timbaland. Coincidence, or something else? What gives?

4. James Hetfield (Metallica)

His band has the word *metal* right in their name. That comes with a big responsibility, in my eyes. Ever notice they started putting out ballads that went to the top of the charts and made them millions? Where is the metal? On the floor with your chopped-off locks?

5. Aerosmith

Take a look at their first album. Tons of hair. Then they became another band that found ballads to be lucrative. Is there a connection? I will say that Steven and Joe have a little hair left, but the rest of the guys look like my accountant....

6. Bruce Dickinson (Iron Maiden)

This guy is one of the true metal greats but somehow he grew up, his hairline started receding, and he finally cut his hair. I was never a fan of his bangs, but still ...

Jason Baker has been an editor for The Colbert Report *since the beginning of the series in 2005. He has performed on the show a couple of times as the Resident Rocker. He started his career twenty years ago as a recording engineer and moved into video editing when the non-linear craze started. He was the lead singer of Sacred Cow, which played throughout New England in the 90s. He lives in a purple house in Connecticut with his girlfriend Leni and three cats. And he is a longhair for life . . .*

Masters of Reality: 12 Heavy Metal Reality Shows

1. *Remaking Vince Neil*

Neil cleans up, works out, and gets plastic surgery for a new solo career.

2. *Celebrity Rehab*

Seth Binzer of Crazy Town goes through withdrawal in public.

3. *Celebrity Rehab 2*

Steven Adler of Guns N' Roses and Tawny Kitaen of Whitesnake videos do the same.

4. Bret Michaels and the *Rock of Love* franchise

Bret's been looking for love in all the wrong places for three seasons.

5. *Rock of Love: Charm School*

Sharon Osbourne teaches young ladies how to act in public.

6. *The Osbournes*

Ozzy Osbourne channels Ozzie Nelson and a nation swoons.

7. *Gene Simmons Family Jewels*

Gene Simmons channels Ozzy Osbourne with normal kids.

8. *'Til Death Do Us Part: Carmen and Dave Uncensored*

Newlyweds Carmen Electra and Dave Navarro help invent TMZ.

9. *Rock Star: Supernova*

Tommy Lee and Dave Navarro get paid to do their business on TV. Searching for a singer, you know?

10. *Tommy Lee Goes to College*

Tommy Lee gets schooled in what it's like to be a dork again.

11. *Battleground Earth*

Dude, Tommy Lee and rapper Ludacris solve global warming, yo.

12. *Supergroup*

Ted Nugent, Scott Ian, Evan Seinfeld, Jason Bonham, and Sebastian Bach channel the Monkees.

11 Notable Cameos in Heavy Metal Videos

1. Milton Berle

"Round and Round"—Ratt

2. Donald Trump

"Mr. Big Stuff"—Precious Metal

3. Sam Kinison

"Bad Medicine"—Bon Jovi

4. Kerry King (Slayer)

"No Sleep Till Brooklyn"—Beastie Boys
Kerry's in the gorilla suit.

5. Michael Berryman

"Home Sweet Home"—Mötley Crüe

6. Bill Wyman
"Eat the Rich"—Motörhead

7. Jon Bon Jovi and Richie Sambora
"Somebody Save Me (Version 2)"—Cinderella

8. Doc McGhee
"I Love It Loud"—Kiss

9. Thora Birch
"Eat You Alive—Limp Bizkit

10. Evan Rachel Wood
"Heart-Shaped Glasses"—Marilyn Manson

11. Gary Oldman
"Since I Don't Have You"—Guns N' Roses

Heavy Mental: 22 Fictitious and Parody Bands

1. Spinal Tap
Never heard of 'em.

2. Green Jellÿ
These comedy rockers perform songs including "Cereal Killer" and "Misadventures of Shitman" and have had, by their count, more than two hundred members since they were formed in 1981. They were warned by the manufacturers of Jell-O to change their name, so they went with Green Jellÿ, which they say is still pronounced Jell-O.

3. Dethklok
The animated band on the hit series *Metalocalypse*. The flesh-and-blood version did a short tour with Brendan Small on vocals and guitar, Mike Kennealy on guitar, Bryan Beller on bass, and Gen Hoglan on drums.

4. Insidious Torment
Their songs include "The Great Cocks of Rock and Roll," "Dinosaurs of Rock," and "Space Marine Death Machine."

5. Deathtongue
The metal band featured in the *Bloom County* comic strip.

6. Steel Panther (formerly Metal Skool)
Glam metal cover/parody band who have a residency at the Key Club on the Sunset Strip. Special guests who have joined them onstage include Kip Winger (who sang "Don't Stop Believing") and Billy Ray Cyrus, who joined them on "Rebel Yell." They were also the house band on the *Gene Simmons Family Jewels* roast of the Demon. Lead singer Ralph Saenz is a former singer of L.A. Guns, and also flaps his gums for the Van Halen tribute band Atomic Punks.

7. Limozeen
A band hailing from the country of "Strong Badia," and the brainchild of an Internet comedy site.

8. Taranchula
Another Strong Badian metal band, who only perform two songs.

9. Massacration
A parody band started by the Brazilian comedy duo Hermes & Renato.

10. Alice Bowie
The glam metal performer introduced on *Cheech & Chong's Wedding Album* in 1974, whose song "Earache My Eye" was a minor radio hit.

11. Bloodhag
This "edu-core" band performs short metal songs about science-fiction authors and only perform at libraries. Their tunes include "Thomas Pynchon," "Iain M. Banks," and "Robert Silverburg."

12. Whistlecore
One-man black metal/experimental band from Texas whose only instrument is a whistle.

13. Goatkill
According to the band's MySpace page, "Goatkill started in 1984 as a 123-piece trip-hop, grindhouse experiment-core band, striving for the raunchiest music possible. Over the course of time, 121 members of what was then called Sarcophagus were struck by an ice meteor that was said to come from Neptune. The remaining

2 members, Bork and the Farmer, decided it was best to move forth and continue making 'music.'"

14. Knife the Puppets
This death metal/grindcore band hails from Rockwall, Texas, and made their splash on a website out to "destroy music."

15. Evil Scarecrow
Theatrical U.K. band who have opened for Gwar and Cradle of Filth. According to band member Brother Pain, "You have to see this band even if you don't like heavy metal . . . or music . . . or going out! It'll be a night you'll remember for weeks."

16. Apologetix
This Christian band rewrites metal standards with a religious twist. Their songs include "It Wasn't Ain't (in the Bible)," a takeoff on "Livin' Lovin' Maid (She's Just a Woman)" and "Born-Again Child," otherwise known as "Born to Be Wild."

17. Psychostick
Comedy band who made news when they sought funding for their CD by asking fans to send them $50 apiece, in exchange for which Psychostick would mention their name in a song, tentatively titled "400 Thank Yous."

18. Bad News
Appeared on the British comedy show *The Comic Strip Presents* in 1983.

19. Buddhist Priest
Honolulu, Hawaii–based cover band fronted by Burgher Kinge ("Like Meat Loaf, only metal!"). Claim to have played with the biggest names in metal, "who ALL stole [our] material."

20. Scatterbrain
Risen from the ashes of New York hardcore band Ludachrist, the band does covers of "Earache My Eye" and "Mama Said Knock You Out," dresses in chicken suits to sing Southern rock, and perform medleys of Mozart and Motörhead.

21. Steel Dragon
The band Mark Wahlberg joins in the film *Rock Star*, loosely based on Judas Priest.

22. Vesuvius
The rock band Rainn Wilson's character used to play drums for in the film *The Rocker*.

IØ THINGS RØNNIE JAMES DIØ IS ØLDER THAN

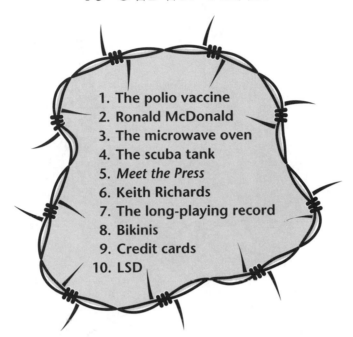

1. The polio vaccine
2. Ronald McDonald
3. The microwave oven
4. The scuba tank
5. *Meet the Press*
6. Keith Richards
7. The long-playing record
8. Bikinis
9. Credit cards
10. LSD

Ted Nugent by the Numbers

1. Number of bullets I own: at last count, 657,329
2. Number of big game animals I've killed: 3,497 (four more just tonight)
3. Magazines that have banned me: 1 (*Rolling Stone*)
4. Pounds of illicit drugs I flushed down backstage toilets in the '70s: over 500
5. Number of Gibson Byrdland guitars I'm currently training: 21
6. Number of PRS guitars I own: 9
7. Number of Gibson Les Pauls I own: 9
8. Number of guitars I own: 47
9. Number of media interviews I give annually: From 1,000 to 1,300
10. Number of *Sports Illustrated* models I could have done a better job preparing for their paint-on bikinis: All of 'em
11. Numbers of hippies I've caused to go insane and check themselves into a mental hospital: At least 3 that I know of

12. Number of times I tell my wife and children that I love them: Immeasurable
13. Number of awards I've been presented: Many, including the James Fenimore Cooper Spiritual Literary Award; the Taurus Patriot Award; Father of the Year; 101st Airborne Patriot Award; Golden Moose People's Choice Award for Ted Nugent Spirit of the Wild TV show (four times and counting); *New York Times* Top 10 Best Seller; Outdoor Channel Viewer Favorite Show Host; 36 Million Selling Gold & Platinum Album Awards; Conservationist of the Year by the Michigan Legislature; Number One Rock Song for "Stranglehold" on numerous radio shows; Arbor Day Foundation Conservationist of the Year; *Outdoor Life* Top 25 Most Influential in Hunting and Fishing; *Los Angeles Times* Top 10 Book Hotlist; Number One Hunt Partner by North American Hunting Club; Muzzy Tall Man Award; ATV Image Award; Man of the Year by Michigan Recreation & Parks Association; and more . . .
14. Number of chain saws I own that are currently inoperable: 11 (operable: 3)
15. Number of funerals my song "Fred Bear" has been played at: Hundreds
16. Number of gay men I've turned on to pussy: Untold masses
17. Number of lesbians I've turned on to gentlemanly romance: Numerous
18. Number of concerts I've played: 6,009
19. Number of women my wife has allowed to sleep with us: 0
20. Number of knives I have on my person at any given moment: At least 3
21. Number of trees I've planted so far in my lifetime: More than 50,000
22. Number of guitar strings I've changed or broken: More than 24,000
23. Pounds of pure venison I've killed and donated to homeless shelters: Over 3 tons
24. Number of dying children I've taken on their last hunt: 11
25. Number of free concert tickets I've donated to U.S. military heroes: Thousands
26. Number of joints I've smoked: 0
27. Number of beers I've consumed in my lifetime: 3
28. Things I'm allergic to: Banjos, unloaded guns, dull knives, Michael Moore, illogic
29. Number of *New York Times* best-selling books I've written: 3
30. Number of animal rights clowns I've personally arrested: 1
31. Number of animal rights clowns I've converted into hunters: Many
32. Number of anti-gun clowns I've turned into NRA members: Hundreds
33. Number of miles I've traveled in pursuit of my American musical dream: Over 4 million

34. Number of bulldozers I've owned: 1; destroyed: 2
35. Number of band members who couldn't keep up with me and blew up: 56
36. Number of kids Ted Nugent Kamp for Kids has introduced to the great outdoors: Over 2,000
37. Number of bows I own: 99
38. Number of haircuts since 1967: 0
39. Number of felony arrests I've assisted in: 6
40. Number of U.S. flag–draped coffins I've saluted: Too many
41. Number of negligent discharges I'm guilty of: None of your damn business
42. Number of firearms I own: 299
43. Number of machine guns I own: None of your damn business
44. Number of liberals I've forced to admit they wouldn't defend their own lives on TV: 1
45. Number of albums I've dedicated to Bernie Goetz: 1
46. Number of albums I've dedicated to Rosa Parks: 2
47. Number of acres of sacred wildlife habitat that I own: 2,200
48. Number of professional off-road races I've competed in: 16
49. Number of races I've won: 3
50. Number of races where I crashed violently in my attempt to win: 4
51. Number of cool-ass cars and trucks I own: 11
52. Number of flat-out laps at the Indy 500 track I rode with Parnelli Jones: 4
53. Number of trespassers I've run off my property at gunpoint while screaming violently: 4
54. Number of trees I've climbed to ambush deer: around 11,000
55. Number of arrows I've shot: A million
56. Number of sunrises and sunsets I've cherished: Approximately 60,000
57. Number of beloved dogs, cats, and horses I've had to bury: 14
58. Number of years I've served on the NRA board of directors: 16
59. Number of children's and military charities I donate to annually: Dozens

With over 35 million albums sold and more media face-time than most active politicians, Ted Nugent has earned his status as an American icon. Acclaimed for his bold, insightful commentary on issues ranging from the American dream to biodiversity, Nugent is a regular guest on top-rated programs like Howard Stern, Glenn Beck, Dennis Miller, The O'Reilly Factor, Hannity & Colmes, Rush Limbaugh, *and more. Ted Nugent is also author of the* New York Times *best sellers* Ted White & Blue: The Nugent Manifesto *and* God, Guns and Rock 'n' Roll, *and is currently serving his fifth term on the board of directors of the NRA.*

ACKNOWLEDGMENTS

Thanks to my family, who are always so supportive of me; Howard Thompson, for the biggest of hookups (cheers, mate!); Lemmy for being fucking Lemmy; Todd Singerman and Eddie Rocha for helping me get the job done; all my celebrity contributors, who let us see into their lives in yet another way; David Orbach for all the research material and for being my best friend, and Deb Cohn-Orbach for all the kind indulgence and being my best friend's wife; my editor, Mike "Sharky" Edison, for knowing what a great job I could do with this and making damn sure I did it; Cliff Mott for bringing all this weird shit to life; Hanna Toresson for making me look so metal; Jessica Burr for being a true comrade; Polly Watson for helping me look like even more of a genius; everyone at Backbeat Books; Victoria Luther, for showing me the long and short of things; Lainie Speiser, Aria Giovanni, Brian Gross, April Arceo, Riss Friend, and the Spread Group; Linda Peterson (for helping me bag the big one); Mark DeMaio; Janine Kloiber and Metal Circle Music; Vince Edwards and Metal Blade Records; Giovanna Melchiorre and Koch Records; Kyle Kraszewski and MRV Music; Bryan Mechutan and Radical Records; Carla Rhodes; Donna Lupie for being a doll; Lara Turchinsky for her encouragement and inspiration; Anthony Maniscalco for giving this book a sound track; James Sasser for remembering the Coop; every bartender who kept me greased during this project; and last but not least myself, for keeping yet another editor happy.

BIBLIOGRAPHY

Baddeley, Gavin, *Lucifer Rising: Sin, Devil Worship & Rock 'N' Roll* (Plexus, 1999).

Beaujon, Andrew, *Body Piercing Saved My Life* (Da Capo, 2006).

Bream, Jon, *Whole Lotta Led Zeppelin: The Illustrated History of the Heaviest Band of All Time* (Voyageur Press, 2008).

Buell, Bebe, with Victor Bockris, *Rebel Heart: An American Rock 'n' Roll Journey* (St. Martins Press, 2001).

Case, George, *Jimmy Page: Magus, Musician, Man* (Hal Leonard, 2007).

Christe, Ian, *Sound of the Beast: The Complete Headbanging History of Heavy Metal* (Harper Entertainment, 2003).

Cole, Richard, with Richard Turbo, *Stairway to Heaven: Led Zeppelin Uncensored* (Harper, 1992).

Demorest, Steve, *Alice Cooper* (Popular Library, 1974).

Des Barres, Pamela, *Rock Bottom: Dark Moments in Music Babylon* (Abacus, 1997).

Konow, David, *Bang Your Head: The Rise and Fall of Heavy Metal* (Three Rivers Press, 2002).

Lee, Tommy, and Mick Mars, Vince Neil, and Nikki Sixx with Neil Strauss, *The Dirt: Confessions of the World's Most Notorious Rock Band* (Regan Books, 2002).

Moynihan, Michael, and Didrik Soderlund, *Lords of Chaos: The Bloody Rise of the Satanic Metal Underground* (Feral House, 1998).

Mudrian, Albert, *Choosing Death: The Improbable History of Death Metal & Grindcore* (Feral House, 2004).

Quisling, Erik and Austin Williams, *Straight Whisky: A Living History of Sex, Drugs and Rock 'n' Roll on the Sunset Strip* (Bonus Books, 2003).

Shea, Stuart, *Rock & Roll's Most Wanted: The Top 10 Book of Lame Lyrics, Egregious Egos and Other Oddities* (Brassey's, 2002).

Slash, with Anthony Bozza, *Slash* (Harper, 2007).

Stenning, Paul, *The Band That Time Forgot: The Complete Unauthorised Biography of Guns N' Roses* (Chrome Dreams, 2004).

Strong, Martin C., *The Great Metal Discography* (Interlink Books, 1999).

Weinstein, Deena, *Heavy Metal: The Music and Its Culture* (Da Capo, 2000).